THE

PRAYER
MINISTRY OF THE
CHURCH

WATCHMAN NEE

Living Stream Ministry
Anaheim, California • www.lsm.org

First Edition, March 1995.

ISBN 0-87083-860-1

Published by

Living Stream Ministry
2431 W. La Palma Ave., Anaheim, CA 92801 U.S.A.
P. O. Box 2121, Anaheim, CA 92814 U.S.A.

Printed in the United States of America

99 00 01 02 03 04 / 13 12 11 10 9 8 7 6 5 4

CONTENTS

PREFACE TO THE CHINESE EDITION

This book contains five messages concerning prayer. The title is taken from the first chapter. Through these messages we hope that God's children will learn to pray with His eternal purpose as the center and learn to carry out the responsibility and authority God has given the church to withstand Satan's attack against prayer. May God gain prayer warriors to co-labor with Him.

The Taiwan Gospel Book Room

CHAPTER ONE

THE PRAYER MINISTRY OF THE CHURCH

"Moreover if your brother sins against you, go, reprove him between you and him alone. If he hears you, you have gained your brother. But if he does not hear you, take with you one or two more, that by the mouth of two or three witnesses every word may be established. And if he refuses to hear them, tell it to the church; and if he refuses to hear the church also, let him be to you just like the Gentile and the tax collector. Truly I say to you, Whatever you bind on the earth shall have been bound in heaven, and whatever you loose on the earth shall have been loosed in heaven. Again, truly I say to you that if two of you are in harmony on earth concerning any matter for which they ask, it will be done for them from My Father who is in the heavens. For where there are two or three gathered into My name, there am I in their midst" (Matt. 18:15-20). These few verses can be divided into two sections. Verses 15-17 are one section, while verses 18-20 are another section. If we read them carefully, we will find the relationship between the two sections. Verses 15-17 cover one specific thing, one particular thing, while verses 18-20 cover the general principle. Verses 15-17 mention one specific case that needs to be dealt with, while verses 18-20 cover a general principle which one should diligently learn. Although the case in verses 15-17 is mentioned first and the principle in verses 18-20 is mentioned second, the words in verses 18-20 are more important than the words in verses 15-17. In other words, the first section covers a specific case, while the second section covers a general principle, a great principle. The way to deal with the case in the first section is based on the principle covered in the second section. The second section is the foundation; the first section merely carries out a matter based on that foundation. In verses 15-17, the Lord Jesus tells us what should be done when a brother has sinned against another brother. The first thing that should be done is to reprove the sinning brother. If he will not listen, the brother who has been sinned against should bring one or two more to reprove him. If he will still not listen, then the church should be told. If he refuses to hear the church, he should be considered a Gentile and a tax collector. After the Lord Jesus mentioned this case, He said, "Truly I say to you...." He meant that one should act in this way because these are crucial matters and because this is an important principle. This is the basis for saying that verses 18-20 are the foundation of verses 15-17.

We are not speaking about the case in verses 15-17. We are trying to consider the broad principle from this one matter. We have to see that we should not only handle a brother's offenses against us in this way but also thousands of other things. Now we want to consider what God intends for us to know in the second section.

THE EARTH CONTROLS HEAVEN

In verse 18 the Lord says, "Truly I say to you, Whatever you bind on the earth shall have been bound in heaven, and whatever you loose on the earth shall have been loosed in heaven." What is special about this verse? The special thing is that there must be a move on earth before there is a move in heaven. It is not heaven that binds first but the earth that binds first. It is not heaven that looses first but the earth that looses first. After the earth binds, heaven binds; after the earth looses, heaven looses. The move in heaven is controlled by the move on earth. Everything contrary to God has to be bound, and everything in harmony with God has to be released. Everything, whether it is something to be bound or loosed, should have its binding or its loosing originate from the earth. The move on the earth precedes the move in heaven. The earth controls heaven.

We can see how the earth controls heaven from a few cases in the Old Testament. When Moses was on the mountain, the Israelites won every time he raised his hands, and the

Amalekites won every time he lowered his hands (Exo. 17:9-11). Who decided the victory at the bottom of the mountain? Did God decide or did Moses decide? Brothers and sisters, we have to see God's principle of work and the key to His move. God cannot do what He wants to do unless man wants it. We cannot make God do what He does not want to do, yet we can stop God from doing what He wants to do. The victory was decided by God in heaven, but the victory was decided by Moses before men. Truly, God in heaven wanted the Israelites to win, but if Moses had not raised his hands on earth, the Israelites would have lost. When he raised his hands, the Israelites won. The earth controls heaven.

Ezekiel 36:37 says, "Thus saith the Lord God; I will yet for this be inquired of by the house of Israel, to do it for them; I will increase them with men like a flock." God has a purpose to increase the number of the house of Israel so that the Israelites would increase like a flock. Those who do not know God will say, "If God wants to increase the number of the Israelites like a flock, He could go ahead and do it. Who could stop Him?" But this verse says that God must be inquired of first before He will accomplish it for them. This is a clear principle: Even though God decides on a matter, He will not do it immediately. He would increase the house of Israel only after they inquired of Him. He wants the earth to control heaven.

Isaiah 45:11 has a most peculiar word, "Thus says Jehovah, / The Holy One of Israel and the One who formed him, / Ask Me about the things to come concerning My sons, / And concerning the work of My hands, command Me." Brothers and sisters, is not this word most peculiar? Concerning the sons and the work of His hand, God says that we can command Him. We would almost be afraid to use the word "command." How can man command God? All those who know God realize that man cannot be haughty before Him. But God Himself says, "Concerning My sons, / And concerning the work of My hands, command Me." This is the earth controlling heaven. It does not mean that we force God to do what He does not want to do. Rather, it means that we can command God to do what He wants to do. This is our position.

After we know God's will, we can say to Him, "God, we want You to do this. We are determined that You should do this. God, You must do this." We can utter such strong and powerful prayers before God. We have to ask God to open our eyes to see the kind of work He is doing in this age. In this age all His work is based on this position. Heaven may want to accomplish something, but heaven will not do it alone; heaven waits for the earth to do it first, and then heaven does it. Although the earth stands in the second place, at the same time, it also stands in the first place. The earth must move before heaven will move. God wants the earth to move heaven.

HARMONY OF WILL

Some may ask why God would want the earth to control heaven. If we want to understand this, we have to remember that our God is limited by time. Time refers to the section between the two eternities. There is an eternity past and an eternity future. Between these two eternities, there is time. Within this section called time, God is limited. He cannot work as freely as He wants to. This is a limitation God encountered in the creation of man. According to Genesis 2, God gave man a free will when He created him. God has a will, and man has a will. Whenever man's will is not one with God's will, God is limited. In this room, there is a table, chair, floor, and ceiling. If a man comes in, he can do whatever he wants and not be restricted. The table, chair, floor, and ceiling will not be able to restrict him. God is a powerful God; He can do anything. If the earth was filled with spiritless material, God would be without restriction. But one day, God created man. The man He created was not like a piece of stone or wood; he was not a table or a chair which could be placed here or there by God at will. The man that God created had a free will. Man could choose to obey God's word and he also could choose to disobey His word. God did not create a man who was obligated to obey Him. He created a man with a free will, one who could obey or disobey His word. After God created a man with a free will, His power was limited by this man. He could no longer act according to what He wanted. He had to ask whether man wanted the same thing and whether he was willing to do the same thing. God cannot treat man like a stone, a piece of wood, a table, or a chair, because man has a free will. Since the day God created man, man could choose to allow God's authority to be carried out or to be blocked. This is why we say that within time, the period between the two eternities, God's authority is limited by man.

God is willing to be limited in time because He wants to gain a harmonious will in the second eternity. He wants man's free will to be harmonious with His will. This is a glory to God. If you put a book on the table, it remains on the table. If you put it on the shelf, it remains on the shelf. It is very obedient to you. But even though it is obedient, you are still not satisfied, because it does not have a free will; it is completely passive. God does not want the man He created to be like a book which can be shuffled around at will. Even though God wants man to be fully submissive to Him, He also gave man a free will. God's intention is that man's free will would choose to obey Him. This is a glory to God! In eternity future the free will of man will be joined to God's eternal will. That will be the time for God's eternal will to be fulfilled and for man's free will to become harmonious with God's eternal will. Every man has a free will. In eternity future man still has a free will, but it will stand on God's side. He still has the ability to oppose God, but he will not oppose Him. Hallelujah! Even though man will have the freedom to oppose God, he will not oppose Him. He will do what God wants. This harmony of will is a glory to God!

In eternity future, although man's will is free, it will be in conformity to God's will, and there will be no will that is not subordinate to God's authority. However, in time, God is limited by man. Man does not do what God wants, or man does only a little of what God wants. God may want something to be big, yet man may want it to be small. Or God may want something to be small, yet man may want it to be big. God has no freedom at all! God's move is controlled by man in time. This speaking is in reference to the church. All of God's moves are limited by the church in time because the church represents man in eternity future. The church is standing on the earth today for God's will. If the church comes up to the standard of God's will, He will not be limited. But if it does not come up to the standard of His will, God will be limited. God is doing what He wants to do through the church. Today the church is taking the position that man will take in eternity. Then, even though man's will is free, it will stand completely on the side of God's eternal will. The church is taking that position ahead of time. Just as God will express Himself in eternity through the New Jerusalem, the Lamb's wife, He also is expressing Himself today through the Body of Christ. Although the church has a free will, it submits this will to God's authority as if no other will existed. This allows God to do whatever He wants to do. When the church places its will under God's will today, He will move in the same way that He will in eternity; He will move as if no other will were opposing Him. This is a glory to God!

Now we can see the church's position before God. We cannot make the church so low by suggesting that it is merely a meeting. No, the church is a group of people who have been redeemed by the blood, who have been regenerated by the Holy Spirit, who have committed themselves to God's hand, and who are willing to take God's will, do His will, and stand for God on earth for the sake of maintaining His testimony.

We have to see that God works according to a law. Since there is free will on earth, God will not annul man by His own will. Brothers and sisters, do not think that this is a strange thing. This is a fact. God is in heaven. Yet all His works on earth can be accomplished only when there is a will on earth that agrees with and decides to do the works. He will not put aside man's will on earth. He will not usurp man's will on earth and act independently. Everything related to Him can be accomplished only when there is a will on earth that cooperates with Him. When the earth works, God works. When the earth decides, God acts. God must have man's will in harmony with His will. This harmony in will is a great glory to God!

THREE GREAT PRINCIPLES

We have said that God has a will for everything. Yet God does not act independently; He will not do anything by Himself. Even though God has a will, He wants the free will on earth to echo His will before He does anything. If there is only a will in heaven, God will not move. The heavenly move is accomplished on earth only when the earth wants the same thing as heaven. Today this is called the ministry of the church. Brothers and sisters, the ministry of the church is not only the preaching of the gospel. This does not mean that we should not preach the gospel; it means that the ministry of the church is not merely the preaching of the gospel. The ministry of the church is to bring the will in heaven to earth. How does the church bring the will in heaven to earth? It is by prayer on earth. Prayer is not as small and insignificant as some may think. It is not something that is dispensable. Prayer is a work. Prayer is the church saying to God, "God, we want Your will." Prayer is the church knowing God's heart and opening its mouth to ask for what is in God's heart. If the church does not do this, it does not have much use on earth.

Many prayers for spiritual edification, prayers for fellowship, and prayers for supplication cannot replace prayers which are in the nature of work or ministry. If all your prayers are prayers for spiritual edification, fellowship, and supplication, they are too small. A prayer which is in the nature of work or ministry is one in which you stand on God's side, wanting what God wants. Brothers and sisters, if a prayer is uttered according to God's will, it is the most powerful thing. For the church to pray means that it finds out God's will and speaks out this will. Prayer is not just asking God for something. For the church to pray means that it stands on God's side to declare that man wants what God wants. If the church declares this, the declaration will be effectual.

Now let us consider three great principles in ministerial prayer from Matthew 18:18-20.

Speaking Out God's Will

In verse 18 the Lord says, "Whatever you bind on the earth

shall have been bound in heaven, and whatever you loose on the earth shall have been loosed in heaven." Who is the "you" here? It is the church because verse 17 mentions the church, and verse 18 is a continuation of verse 17. Whatever the church binds on earth will be bound in heaven, and whatever the church looses on earth will be loosed in heaven. This is a very important principle: today God works through the church. God cannot do anything at will; He has to do everything through the church. Without going through the church, God cannot do anything. Brothers and sisters, this is a very sober principle. God cannot do anything by Himself today. There is a free will besides His will. If this will does not cooperate with Him, He cannot do anything. The amount of power that the church has expresses the amount of power that God has because His power is expressed through the church. God has placed Himself in the church. The height and extent that the church reaches is the height and extent that God's power reaches. If the power of the church is small and restricted, God cannot express the height or extensiveness of His power. The water department's reservoir may be great, but if you have only a small tap in your house, a great amount of water will not flow out. If you want more water in your house, you have to install a larger pipe. Today the capacity of the church determines the degree to which God's power is expressed. This can be seen from God's expression in Christ; the capacity of Christ is the degree of the manifestation of God. Today God is expressed in the church; the capacity of the church determines the degree of the expression of God and also the amount of knowledge one can have about God.

God wants to do many things on earth today. But He must have the church stand on His side before He can accomplish these things through the church. God cannot do what He wants to do by Himself; He has to do it with the cooperation of the church. The church is the means through which God expresses Himself. Let me repeat: the church is like a water tap. If the tap is small, the amount of water flowing through the tap will not be great, even if there is as much water as the Yangtze River. God truly wants to work in heaven, but He has to wait for the earth to move before He can work. There are many things that God wants to bind in heaven, and there are many things that God wants to loose in heaven. God wants to see many people, objects, and things contrary to Him bound, and He wants to see many spiritual, valuable, beneficial, and holy things that are of Him loosed. The question is whether or not there are men on earth to bind what God wants to bind and loose what God wants to loose. He wants the earth to control heaven. God wants the church to control heaven.

This by no means says that God is not omnipotent. God is indeed omnipotent, but He needs a channel on earth before He can manifest His omnipotence. We cannot increase God's power, but we can hinder His power. Man cannot increase God's power, but he can block His power. We cannot ask God to do what He does not want to do, but we can limit what He wants to do. We cannot ask God to do something that He is not willing to do, yet we can stop Him from doing something He wants to do. Brothers and sisters, have you seen this? There is a power in the church which puts God's power under its control. It can allow God to do what He wants to do, and it can stop God from doing what He wants to do. Our eyes have to be opened to see the future. One day God will expand the church to become the New Jerusalem. God's glory will be manifested from the church without any hindrance. Today He wants the church to first loose on earth before He looses in heaven. He wants the church to first bind on earth before He binds in heaven. Heaven will not take the initiative to work; it follows the earth's work. God will not take the initiative to work; He follows the church's work. Brothers and sisters, since this is the case, how great is the responsibility of the church!

We have seen that Matthew 18:15-17 speaks of a particular case and that the great principle is given in the following verses. When a brother sins against another, he may not confess his sins or mistakes. When the church reproves him, he still may not listen. If this happens, the church will consider him as the Gentile and the tax collector. The sinning brother may say, "Who are you? How can you make me as the Gentile and the tax collector? I will just stop coming to your meeting. If I cannot come to this place, there are many other places I can go to." However, what does the Lord Jesus say after this? "Truly I say to you, Whatever you bind on the earth shall have been bound in heaven, and whatever you loose on the earth shall have been loosed in heaven." Hence, if the church decides to consider a man a Gentile, God in heaven will consider him a Gentile also. If the church considers a man a tax collector, God in heaven will consider him a tax collector also. In other words, God will do in heaven what the church does on earth. If the church considers a brother a Gentile and a tax collector, God in heaven will consider the same brother a Gentile and a tax collector. Not only does this case follow the principle, a thousand other matters follow the same principle. This case is only an example. It shows us how much the church can do. Then it shows us the greatness of the principle.

The church is God's chosen vessel. God has placed His will in this vessel so that it will declare God's will on earth. When the earth wants something, heaven also wants it. When the church wants something, God also wants it. Hence, if God's demand is rejected in the church, God will not be able to accomplish what He wants to accomplish in heaven.

Many brothers and sisters are bearing a burden day and night. They are bearing the burden because they have not prayed. Once the tap is turned on, water flows out. Once it is turned off, the water is blocked. Is the water pressure strong when water is released or when it is blocked? We all know that when water is released, the pressure decreases. When water is blocked, the pressure increases. When the church prays, it is like turning on the tap; the more the tap is turned, the less the pressure becomes. If the church does not pray, it is like a tap being turned off with pressure building up. When God wants to accomplish something, He puts a burden in a brother, sister, or the whole church. If the church prays and fulfills its duty, it will feel relieved. The more the church prays, the more relieved it will feel. As it prays once, twice, five times, ten times, or twenty times, it feels more and more relieved. If the church does not pray, it will feel stuffed and burdened. If the church continues to not pray, it will suffocate to death. Brothers and sisters, if you feel heavy and pressed within, you have not fulfilled your ministry before God; God's pressure is upon you. Try to pray for half an hour or an hour; the pressure will be released, and you will feel relieved.

What then is the prayer ministry of the church? It is God telling the church what He wants to do and the church praying on earth what God wants to do. This prayer is not asking God to accomplish what we want Him to do, but asking God to accomplish what He Himself wants to do. Brothers and sisters, the church's responsibility is to declare God's will on earth. On earth the church declares for God, "This is what I want." If the church fails in this matter, it will not be of much use in God's hand. Even if everything else is good, it will not be of much use if it fails in this matter. The greatest use of the church lies in the fact that it stands for God's will to be done on earth.

The Harmony in the Holy Spirit

We have seen that the church should bind what God wants to bind and loose what God wants to loose. How does the church bind and loose? The Lord tells us in verse 19, "Again, truly I say to you that if two of you are in harmony on earth concerning any matter, any matter that they ask will be done for them from My Father who is in the heavens" (alternate translation). Verse 18 concerns earth and heaven. Verse 19 also concerns earth and heaven. In verse 18, when the earth binds, heaven binds, and when the earth looses, heaven looses. Verse 19 says that whatever one asks on earth will be fulfilled by the Father in heaven. The emphasis of the Lord Jesus here is not on asking in harmony, but on being in harmony concerning any matter and then asking concerning such matters. According to the original language, "any matter" belongs to both "in harmony" and "that they ask." The Lord's intention is not to tell men to pray for a certain matter in harmony, but to be in harmony concerning any matter. If we are in harmony concerning any matter, then our Father in heaven will accomplish whatever we ask concerning a particular matter. This is the oneness of the Body, the oneness in the Holy Spirit.

A man would feel quite extraordinary if his flesh had not

been dealt with because even heaven listens to him. If you are not in the oneness of the Holy Spirit and not praying in the harmony of the Holy Spirit, do you think heaven will listen to you? If you pray this way, heaven will not bind what you bind and loose what you loose. To have heaven loose and bind is not something you can do by yourself. To think that you can do this by yourself is very foolish. The Lord says, "If two of you are in harmony on earth concerning any matter, any matter that they ask will be done for them from My Father who is in the heavens." This means that if two persons are in harmony concerning any matter, as harmonious as music, then whatever they ask will be done for them from the heavenly Father. This kind of prayer requires the constitution of the Holy Spirit in the praying ones. God has to take you to the point where you deny what you want and want only what God wants, and another brother has to be brought by God to the point where he denies what he wants and wants only what God wants. When both you and the brother are brought to this point and are as harmonious as music, whatever you ask will be done for you from the heavenly Father. Brothers and sisters, do not think that as long as you agree in your opinions that your prayers will be answered. Those who have the same opinions often have friction between them. A sameness in goal does not guarantee that there will be no friction. Perhaps two people are trying to preach the gospel. But while they are preaching, they argue about it. Perhaps two people are trying to help others, but while they are helping others, they have friction between themselves. Sameness in goal does not guarantee that there will be harmony. We have to realize that it is impossible to have harmony in the flesh. When our natural life is dealt with by the Lord, when one is living in the Holy Spirit and the other is also living in the Holy Spirit and both are living in Christ, there is harmony, the same views, and the prayer in one accord.

There are two aspects to this truth. On the one hand, there is the harmony concerning any matter. On the other hand, there is the prayer concerning any matter. God must bring us to this point. Christian harmony can be found only in the Body of Christ; it cannot be found anywhere else. Harmony is something found in the Body of Christ. Only in the Body of Christ is there no striving, and only in the Body of Christ is there harmony. When our natural life is dealt with by the Lord, and we are brought to the point where we truly know the Body of Christ, we will be in harmony. Then when we come together to pray, our prayer will be in harmony. When we stand on a harmonious ground, the things we do will be in harmony. When we are in harmony in the things we see, we can be the mouthpiece of God's will. Brothers and sisters, when you are about to pray for certain things, and you hold a different view, you have to be careful; you may make mistakes. But if the whole church gathers together and is in harmony concerning a certain matter, that matter must be what heaven intends to accomplish. We have to trust the church.

We must remember that prayer is not the first thing. Prayer is something that comes after harmony. If the church is to have this kind of ministerial prayer on earth, every brother and sister must learn before the Lord to deny the fleshly life. Otherwise, nothing will avail. The Lord's word is very significant. He does not say that the Father will answer if we pray in His name. Neither does He say that the Father will answer if He prays for us. He says, "If two of you are in harmony on earth concerning any matter, any matter that they ask will be done for them from My Father who is in the heavens." If we are in harmony, the heavens will be open to us! If a brother offends another brother, and the church has not yet come in to deal with the offending brother, the offended brother should reprove him with one or two others. Before the church comes in to deal with the offending brother, two brothers should come. This does not mean that the two brothers see things differently from the church. It means that the two brothers have seen it first, and afterward the church sees the same thing. In other words, the two brothers are standing on the ground of the church. The Lord meant that for two of us to be on the earth is for the church to be on the earth. What the church sees is the same as what the two brothers see. This is the result of ministerial prayer. Before they have the same view, they must first be in harmony concerning any matter and must have prayed concerning a certain matter.

The prayer ministry of the church is a prayer on earth that results in a move in heaven. Brothers and sisters, we must remember that the prayer in Matthew 18 can never be covered by prayers that are in the nature of spiritual edification. It can never be covered by personal prayers. We often can ask God for what we lack, and God answers our prayer. There is a place for personal prayers. We often feel that God is near to us. Thank the Lord, He hears prayers that are for spiritual edification. We should not despise this kind of prayer. We admit that it is wrong for a brother or a sister not to receive an answer for his or her prayer, and it is wrong for us not to feel the presence of God. We should pay attention to personal prayers and prayers for our own spiritual edification. This is particularly true for young brothers and sisters. If they do not have these kinds of prayers, they cannot go on properly. However, we must also see that prayers are not just for individuals and for spiritual edification. Prayer is for ministry and work. This prayer is the ministry of the church on earth; it is the work of the church. It is the responsibility that the church bears before God. The prayer of the church is the outlet of heaven. The prayer of the church means that when God wants to do something, the church prays about that matter first so that it can be fulfilled and God's goal can be accomplished.

The ministry of the church is the ministry of the Body of Christ, and the ministry of the Body of Christ is prayer. This prayer is not just for spiritual edification and personal needs but for "heaven." This prayer, for example, tells others that a person has lost his fellowship with God, that he has not listened to the reproof of one brother or even two or three brothers, and that he does not take the judgment of the church. God has to consider him a Gentile and a tax collector. But He will not do this immediately; He has to wait for the church to do it first. God has to wait for the church to judge this brother as a Gentile and a tax collector in its prayer before He will do the same thing in heaven.

If the church takes up this responsibility to pray, it will see that from that day forward his life and spiritual walk will dry up. From that day forward, he will appear to have no part in God. God wants to do this, but He has to wait for the church to pray. God has many things stacked up in heaven. He cannot accomplish any of them because there is no outlet for Him on earth. There are numerous things stacked up in heaven. Yet God cannot resolve them because the church has not exercised its free will to stand on God's side and fulfill God's goal. Brothers and sisters, you have to remember that the highest and greatest work of the church is to be the outlet of God's will. The church becomes the outlet of God's will through prayer. This prayer is not a fragmentary prayer but a prayer that is in the nature of a ministry, a prayer that is in the nature of a work. God gives man vision and opens man's eyes to see His will. When this happens, man takes his place to pray.

The Lord also shows us in these verses that individual prayers do not work. There must be at least two persons. If you do not see this point, you will not understand why the Lord says what He says. All the prayers in the Gospel of John are individual prayers. When John 15:16 records, "Whatever you ask the Father in My name, He may give you," the number of people is not a condition. But in Matthew 18 the number is a condition; there must be at least two persons. The Lord says, "If two of you are in harmony on earth." There must be at least two because this is a question of fellowship. One person cannot accomplish this. One person cannot be God's outlet; there must be two. The principle of two is the principle of the church, the principle of the Body of Christ. Although there are only two in this kind of prayer, the "harmony" is indispensable. The two must be in harmony, and they must stand on the ground of the Body. They must know the Body life. There is only one goal with them, which is to tell God, "We want Your will to be done, in heaven and on earth." When the church prays in this position, whatever it asks will be done for it from the Father who is in the heavens.

Brothers and sisters, when we truly stand on the ground of the church and take up the responsibility of such a ministry of prayer before God, we will see God's will carried out in the church where we are. Otherwise, everything will be in vain. There can be many prayers or few prayers, but the main thing is to have strong prayers. What God does today is measured by the amount of prayer that the church offers. God's power cannot exceed the prayer of the church. The power of God today can at most be as great as the prayer of the church. This does not mean that God's power is limited in heaven. In heaven, God's power is unlimited. But on earth, God's power is manifested to the degree that the church prays. The amount that the church prays will be the measure of the amount that God's power is manifested. Consequently, the church has to learn to pray big prayers and make big requests. The prayer of the church is often very small; it prays only for ordinary problems. This is not enough. The church needs to have big prayers and make big requests. Since the church is coming to such a rich God, there must not be small prayers and small requests. Since the church is coming to such a rich God, there must be great things happening. If the capacity of the church before God is small, it will restrict the power of God from being manifested. We know that the question of the overcomers is not quite resolved, and Satan is not yet thrown into the abyss. God must gain a vessel for His testimony before He can accomplish what He has set out to accomplish. The church must have big prayers to manifest our God. This is the ministry of the church. Brothers and sisters, I do not know whether God can say to us that this church has a ministry of prayer when He passes by our prayer meeting. It is not a question of how often we pray. It is a question of the weight of our prayer. If we see the church's responsibility of prayer, we will see that our prayers are not big enough; we are limiting God and frustrating His work. The church has forsaken its duty! What a sad situation this is!

The issue at stake is this: Can God gain a church that is faithful to its ministry? This depends on whether we are those destined to be disqualified, or whether we are the real vessels of God who will fulfill God's goal. Brothers and sisters, we have to cry out loudly that God is watching to see whether the church is faithful to its ministry. The ministry of the church is prayer—not small prayers, but prayers that pioneer the way for God. God is accomplishing His work. But the church first prays and prepares the way before God finds the way. The church must have big prayers, serious prayers, and strong prayers. Prayer cannot be small before God. If prayers are centered around ourselves, our personal difficulties, and our small losses and gains, it will be difficult to open a way for God's eternal will. Many things should drive us to dig deep. But above all, prayer should drive us to the utmost depth.

For two to be in harmony is not an empty word; it is not a slogan. If we do not know what the Body of Christ is and have not taken this ground, it will be useless even if two hundred people are praying together. If we know the Body of Christ and stand on the proper ground of this Body to deny the flesh, if we do not ask things for ourselves but ask for God's will to be done on earth, we will see that our prayer is in harmony. When this happens, God in heaven will fulfill our prayer on earth.

Please note the precious word in verse 18, "whatever." There is also a precious phrase in verse 19, "concerning any matter." The Lord says, "Whatever you bind on the earth shall have been bound in heaven, and whatever you loose on the earth shall have been loosed in heaven." This means that heaven binds as much as earth binds, and looses as much as earth looses. The capacity in heaven is controlled by the capacity on earth. We should not be afraid that the capacity on earth is too large, because the capacity in heaven is always larger. The capacity on earth can never match the capacity in heaven. Heaven always wants to bind more than the earth binds, and heaven always wants to loose more than the earth looses. The Lord says that whatever we bind on the earth shall have been bound in heaven and whatever we loose on the earth shall have been loosed in heaven. This kind of binding and loosing is not done by individuals; it is done when "two of you are in harmony on earth concerning any matter." Any matter that they ask will be done for them from the Father who is in the heavens. Brothers and sisters, God's

power will be forever greater than our power. The water in
the reservoir is forever greater than the water in our tap.
The water in the well is forever greater than the water in
our bucket. The power in heaven can never be measured by
one's view on earth.

Being Gathered Together

In verse 20 the Lord says, "For where there are two or
three gathered into My name, there am I in their midst."
This is the third principle, the deepest principle. Verse 18 is
a principle, verse 19 is another principle, and verse 20 is a
third principle. The principle in verse 20 is broader than the
principle in verse 19. Verse 19 says, "If two of you are in
harmony on earth concerning any matter, any matter that
they ask will be done for them from My Father who is in the
heavens." Why? "For where there are two or three gathered
into My name, there am I in their midst." Why is there such
a great power on earth? Why is prayer in harmony so
powerful? Why is prayer in harmony of two or three persons
so powerful? It is powerful because whenever we are gathered
together into the Lord's name, the Lord is there! This is the
reason for our harmony. Verse 18 describes the relationship
between the earth and heaven. Verse 19 mentions the prayer
in harmony on earth, and verse 20 tells us how we can have
this harmony.

We are gathered together. We do not choose to meet
together; we are gathered together. There is a difference
between meeting together and being gathered together. Being
gathered together is being gathered by the Lord. We do not
come by ourselves; the Lord has gathered us. Many people
come to the meeting for the sake of observing or spectating;
this will surely not result in anything. But for others, the
Lord is speaking within them, telling them that if they do
not come that day, they will miss something. Those whom
the Lord has gathered this way are gathered together into
the Lord's name; they come for the sake of the Lord's name.
Whenever these brothers and sisters come together, they can
say, "I am here for the Lord's name and for glorifying the
Son. I am not here for myself." When all the brothers and

sisters are gathered together for the Lord's name's sake, there will be oneness and harmony. Thank the Lord. If you come to a meeting for your own sake, there will not be harmony. If you want something, not because you want it but because the Lord wants it, and if you reject something, not because you reject it, but because the Lord rejects it, there will be harmony. God's children are gathered by the Lord into His name. The Lord says, "There am I in their midst." The Lord is leading them in their midst. Since the Lord is leading and enlightening them, and since the Lord is speaking and giving revelation, whatever is bound on the earth is bound in heaven and whatever is loosed on the earth is loosed in heaven. This is because the Lord is doing the binding and the loosing together with the church.

Therefore, we have to learn to deny ourselves before the Lord. Every time He gathers us together in a meeting, we have to learn to seek His glory. Our hearts have to be turned toward His name and desire that His name be exalted above every name and that every idol be cast down. If we do this, He will lead us. Brothers and sisters, this is not a feeling. This is not a theory. This is a fact. If the church is normal, at the end of every meeting, the church will know whether the Lord has been in its midst. When the Lord is in the midst of the church, the church will be rich and strong. During these times, the church can bind and loose. If the Lord is not in its midst, nothing can be done. Only the church can be so strong; individuals can never do this.

May God grant us deeper understanding and deeper lessons in prayer. It is not enough to just have personal prayers and prayers for spiritual edification. There must be prayers that are for the ministry and the work. May the Lord sustain us with power so that every time we gather together we can work in our prayer and fulfill the ministry of the church with our prayer. In this way, the Lord can accomplish what He wants to accomplish.

Chapter Two

"PRAY IN THIS WAY"

"And when you pray, you shall not be like the hypocrites, because they love to pray standing in the synagogues and on the street corners, so that they may be seen by men. Truly I say to you, They have their reward in full. But you, when you pray, enter into your private room, and shut your door and pray to your Father who is in secret; and your Father who sees in secret will repay you. And in praying do not babble empty words as the Gentiles do; for they suppose that in their multiplicity of words they will be heard. Therefore do not be like them, for your Father knows the things that you have need of before you ask Him. You then pray in this way: Our Father who is in the heavens, Your name be sanctified; Your kingdom come; Your will be done, as in heaven, so also on earth. Give us today our daily bread. And forgive us our debts, as we also have forgiven our debtors. And do not bring us into temptation, but deliver us from the evil one. For Yours is the kingdom and the power and the glory forever. Amen. For if you forgive men their offenses, your heavenly Father will forgive you also; but if you do not forgive men their offenses, neither will your Father forgive your offenses" (Matt. 6:5-15).

Ordinarily, when we speak of prayer, we are concerned about answers to prayer. The Lord Jesus' emphasis in these verses is not on answers to prayer but on the reward of prayer. Based on what do we say this? It is based on the word "reward" in verse 5, which is the same word as the "reward" of almsgiving in verse 2 and the "reward" of fasting in verse 16. If the reward of prayer refers to answers to prayer, what do the rewards of almsgiving and fasting refer to? According to its context, "reward" refers to the reward one receives in the kingdom. This shows us that having our prayers answered is secondary; the main thing is receiving reward for our prayer. If our prayers are according to God's will, they will not only be answered, but they will also be remembered and rewarded in the future before the judgment seat. Hence, the prayer mentioned in these verses brings not only an answer today but righteousness as well. In other words, our prayer is our righteousness.

However, the righteousness of prayer does not come from careless prayers, half-hearted prayers, routine prayers, or prayers that issue from impure motives. On the one hand, the Lord teaches us not to pray the way that two kinds of people pray. On the other hand, He shows us a pattern for prayer. First, let us consider the two kinds of prayers which we should not follow.

NOT LIKE THE HYPOCRITES WHO PRAY IN ORDER TO BE SEEN BY MEN

"And when you pray, you shall not be like the hypocrites, because they love to pray standing in the synagogues and on the street corners, so that they may be seen by men. Truly I say to you, They have their reward in full." Prayer is for the purpose of fellowshipping with God and expressing His glory. But hypocrites utilize prayers that are for the glorification of God to glorify themselves. Consequently, they like to pray in the synagogues and on the street corners. They do this in order to be seen by others, because synagogues and street corners are public places, places that men pass by all the time. They do not pray in order to be heard by God but to be heard by men. They want to show themselves off. This kind of prayer is very superficial; it cannot be considered as a prayer to God, and it cannot be considered as fellowship with God. These men cannot expect to receive anything from God, because the motive behind this kind of prayer is to receive glory from men, and because there is no supply reserved before God. They have already received their reward; they have received men's praise. Therefore, in the future kingdom, there will be nothing to remember.

What then should we do when we pray? The Lord said,

"But you, when you pray, enter into your private room, and shut your door and pray to your Father who is in secret; and your Father who sees in secret will repay you." The private room here is a symbol. The synagogues and street corners both refer to open places, while the private room refers to a hidden place. Brothers and sisters, you can find the private room in the synagogues and on the street corners. You can find the private room on the sidewalk and in a car. The private room is the place where you fellowship with God in secret; it is the place where you pray without trying consciously to exhibit your prayer. "Enter into your private room, and shut your door." This means to shut out the world and shut yourself in. In other words, it is to ignore all the outside voices and to pray to God quietly and alone.

When you "pray to your Father who is in secret...your Father who sees in secret will repay you." What a great comfort this is! In order to pray to the Father who is in secret, you need to have faith. Although you do not feel anything outwardly, you have to believe that you are praying to the Father who is in secret! He is in secret, in a place that human eyes cannot see. Yet He is truly there. He does not despise your prayer; He sees you. This shows how much He cares for your prayers. He does not see you and then leave; He will repay you. Brothers and sisters, can you believe this word? If the Lord said that He will repay you, it means that He will repay you. The Lord guarantees that your prayer in secret will not be in vain. If you pray in a proper way, the Father will repay you. Even if there does not appear to be any repayment today, there will be repayment one day. Brothers and sisters, does your prayer in secret pass the test of the Father's seeing in secret? Do you believe that the Father sees you in secret and will repay you?

NOT BABBLING EMPTY WORDS AS THE GENTILES DO

The Lord taught us not only to shut ourselves up in secret when we pray; He also taught us not to "babble empty words as the Gentiles do; for they suppose that in their multiplicity of words they will be heard." The expression "multiplicity of words" in Greek is used to describe the monotonous and repetitious sound that a stammering person makes. Some people repeat the same words monotonously in their prayers. This kind of prayer has sound only; it has no meaning whatsoever. When you stand beside such a person and listen to his prayer, it is as if you are standing by a stream listening to the repetitious and monotonous sound of water tumbling against the rocks. It is like standing on a pebbled street and listening to the repetitious and monotonous sound of wheels rolling across pebbles. They repeat the same words over and over again. They suppose that their prayers will be heard through much repetition. But this kind of prayer is useless; it is not at all effective, and we should not pray in that kind of way.

Brothers and sisters, your prayers should not be sound only, which do not have meaning. The prayers of many people in the prayer meeting are meaningless. If you do not say Amen when they pray, they condemn you for not being one with them. But if you say Amen to their prayer, they will repeat the same words over and over again. They do not pray to fulfill some goals but to generate some commotion. Their prayers are not for the purpose of releasing the burden but for finishing up their speech. Many prayers are offered as a result of man's influence, and many words are uttered which are beyond one's desires. These prayers are like the sound of a stream tumbling against the rocks; they are also like the sound of wheels rolling over pebbles. This kind of prayer has sound only, and it is meaningless. We should not be like those who pray this way.

"Therefore do not be like them, for your Father knows the things that you have need of before you ask Him." This shows us that whether or not our prayers will be answered depends on our attitude before God; it also depends on our need. Whether or not prayers are answered depends not on the multiplicity of our words. If we pray for what we do not need, we will not be heard even if we have more words. If our asking is not out of necessity, it is greed and vain asking. God is happy to give us what we need. But He does not want to satisfy the desires that our self craves. Some have said that since God knows what we need, we do not have to ask anymore. This is a foolish word. The purpose of our prayer is not to inform God of something but to show Him our trust, our faith, our dependence, and our wish. Therefore, it is right that we pray. But when we pray, our desire should exceed our words, and our faith should exceed our words.

"PRAY IN THIS WAY"

Now let us consider the prayer that the Lord taught. This prayer is commonly called the Lord's Prayer, but this is wrong. This prayer is not the Lord's own prayer; it is a prayer that the Lord was teaching us. Luke 11 points this out clearly (vv. 1-4). We should learn carefully from this prayer.

The Lord said, "You then pray in this way." He did not say to pray with these words. If He had, all we would have to do is repeat these words every time we prayed. No, this is not what the Lord meant. The Lord meant that we should pray in this way. In other words, the Lord was teaching us how to pray; He was not teaching us to imitate His words, but to pray in His way.

Since the beginning of the world, God has been listening to man's prayers. Generation after generation and age after age, men have been praying to God. But it is hard to find some whose prayers are to the point. Many people pay attention to their needs; they do not pay attention to God's needs. This is why the Lord opened His mouth and told us to "pray in this way." To "pray in this way" is something very significant, great, and profound. Brothers and sisters, if we want to learn to pray at all, we have to learn to "pray in this way." This was the first time since God came down to earth to become a man that He told us how to pray and how to pray in a concise way.

The Lord told us that we have to pray to "our Father who is in the heavens." "Father" is a title, a new name by which man addresses God. Prior to this, man called God "the Almighty," "the Most High," "the living God," or "Jehovah." No one dared to call God the "Father." This was the first time the word "Father" was used. This shows us clearly that this prayer is for saved ones, those who have eternal life already. When a man is saved, he can call God the Father.

Only those who are begotten of God are the children of God, and only they can call God the Father. This prayer is directed toward "our Father who is in the heavens." How sweet this is and what a great comfort it is. Originally, only our Lord Jesus could call God the Father. But in these verses, He instructed us to call God our Father. This is a great revelation. If God had not loved us and given us His only begotten Son, how could we call God our Father? Thank God that His Son has died and risen for us so that we can become God's children and receive a new position. From now on we can pray to our Father who is in the heavens. How intimate, free, and uplifting this is. May the Spirit of the Lord teach us more and more to know that God is our Father and to believe that the Father is loving and patient. Not only does He want to hear our prayer; He also wants us to share the joy of prayer.

This prayer can be divided into three sections. The first section has to do with the things of God. It is a prayer with three desires concerning God (Matt. 6:9-10). This is the foundation. The second section has to do with us; it is our request for God's protection (vv. 11-13a). The third section is our declaration; it is our praise to God (v. 13b). Let us consider the prayer section by section.

THREE DESIRES CONCERNING GOD

The first section covers three desires concerning God.

The First Desire: "Your Name Be Sanctified"

"Your name be sanctified!" God has an expectation that we all pray for His name to be sanctified by men. His name is exalted among the angels. But on earth, His name is being used in vain; even the idols use His name. When a man takes the name of God in vain, God does not show His wrath by striking him with thunder. He hides Himself, as if He did not exist. When a man takes His name in vain, He does not do anything to deal with him. Yet He wants His children to pray, "Your name be sanctified." Brothers and sisters, if you love God and know Him, you will want His name to be sanctified. If anyone takes God's name in vain, you will feel hurt, your desire will be even stronger, and you will pray even more earnestly: "Your name be sanctified." One day man will sanctify this name and no longer take this name in vain.

"Your name be sanctified!" God's name is not only a title we address with our mouth; it is a great revelation we receive from the Lord. God's name is used in the Bible to designate His revelation to man concerning Himself; it denotes everything we know about Him. God's name speaks of God's nature, and it reveals His fullness. This is not something that man can understand with his soul but something that the Lord reveals to us (John 17:6). The Lord said, "And I have made Your name known to them and will yet make it known, that the love with which You have loved Me may be in them, and I in them" (17:26). This shows us that in order to know God's name, we need the Lord to make it known to us again and again.

"Your name be sanctified!" This is not only our desire but also our worship to the Father. We should give glory to God. We should begin our prayer with praises. Before we can hope to receive mercy and grace from Him, we should give glory to Him. We should allow Him to gain the fullest praise concerning Himself, and then we should receive grace from Him. Brothers and sisters, we have to remember that the main thing and the ultimate goal in our prayer is for God to gain glory.

"Your name be sanctified!" God's name is linked to God's glory. Ezekiel 36 says, "But I had pity for mine holy name, which the house of Israel had profaned among the heathen, whither they went" (v. 21). This means that the house of Israel had not sanctified God's name, so God's name was profaned wherever they went among the heathens. Yet God had pity for His holy name. Our Lord wants us to have this desire. In other words, He wants to glorify His own name through us. God's name must first be sanctified in our hearts before our desire can be turned to something more profound. There must be a deep work of the cross before we can glorify God's name. Otherwise, our desire is not even a desire but only an empty idea. Brothers and sisters, this being the case, how much we need to be dealt with and trimmed.

The Second Desire: "Your Kingdom Come"

What kind of kingdom is this kingdom? If we read the context in Matthew, we will see that this kingdom refers to the kingdom of the heavens. The Lord teaches us to pray, "Your kingdom come." This means that the kingdom of God is in heaven, but the kingdom of God is not on earth. Consequently, we have to pray for God to expand the heavenly sphere to the earth. In the Bible God's kingdom is historical as well as geographical. History has to do with time, while geography has to do with place. According to the Bible, the kingdom of God is more a geographical matter than a historical matter. The Lord said, "If I, by the Spirit of God, cast out the demons, then the kingdom of God has come upon you" (Matt. 12:28). Is this related to history? No, it is something related to geography. The kingdom of God is wherever the Son of God casts out demons. Hence, within this period of time, the kingdom of God is more a matter of geography than a matter of history. Brothers and sisters, if you are filled with a historical concept of the kingdom, you have seen only one side of the truth and not all sides. In the Old Testament, one only finds prophecy concerning the kingdom of the heavens. When the Lord Jesus came, we had the declaration of John the Baptist, who proclaimed that the kingdom of the heavens had drawn near (Matt. 3:1-2). Then the Lord Jesus Himself said that the kingdom of the heavens had drawn near (4:17). They said this because by then there were people who were already of the kingdom of the heavens. By Matthew 13, we have the appearance of the kingdom of the heavens on earth. Today the kingdom of God is wherever God's children cast the demons and their works out by the Spirit of God. In asking us to pray for His kingdom to come, the Lord is looking forward to the time when God's kingdom will fill the whole earth.

"Your kingdom come!" This is not only a desire of the church, but also a responsibility of the church. The church should bring in God's kingdom. In order to bring in God's kingdom, the church has to pay the price to be restricted by heaven and come under heaven's rule. It has to be the outlet for heaven, and it has to allow heaven's authority to be expressed on earth. In order to bring in God's kingdom, the church has to know all the schemes of Satan (2 Cor. 2:11). It has to put on the whole armor of God and stand against the stratagems of the devil (Eph. 6:11), for wherever the kingdom of God is, the devil is cast out. When the kingdom of God rules on earth fully, Satan will be cast into the abyss (Rev. 20:1-3). Since the church has such a tremendous responsibility, Satan will do all he can to attack the church. May the church pray like the saints of old, "O Jehovah, bow Your heavens down and descend" (Psa. 144:5). "Oh that You would rend the heavens, that You would come down" (Isa. 64:1). At the same time, we should say to Satan, "Depart from the earth immediately, and go to the eternal fire which God has prepared for you" (cf. Matt. 25:41).

The Third Desire:
"Your Will Be Done, as in Heaven, So Also on Earth"

The prayer here is "Your will be done, as in heaven, so also on earth." This shows that God's will is done in heaven, but that it is not fully done on earth. God is God; who can stop His will from being done? Can man stop God? Can the devil stop God? No one can stop God. Why then do we have to pray? To answer this question, we have to mention something about the principle of prayer.

In the whole Bible, there are a few basic principles concerning the truth. The principle of prayer is one of these principles. Brothers and sisters, we have to realize that it is wonderful that such a thing as prayer can exist in the Bible. God truly knows our need already. Why then do we need to pray? In man's view, since God is omniscient, there is no need for man to pray. Yet according to the Bible, God needs man's prayer. Prayer means that God wants to do something, yet He will not do it Himself; He will wait for man on earth to pray about it before He does it. God has His will and thoughts. Yet He is waiting for man to pray. God knows our needs, yet He has to wait for man to pray before He will do anything. He will not move by Himself; He will move only after man has prayed. The reason that we need to pray is because God will not do anything by Himself; He has to wait for man to pray before He works. The Lord Jesus was to be born. But there needed to be a Simeon and an Anna to pray for this (Luke 2:25, 36-38). The Holy Spirit was to descend, but it could not descend until the hundred and twenty people prayed for ten days (Acts 1:15; 2:1-2). This is the principle of prayer. Can we through prayer ask God not to do what He wants? No, we cannot. Yet God has to wait for us to pray before He can do what He wants to do. At the time of Ahab, the word of Jehovah came to Elijah clearly, "I will send rain upon the earth." But Elijah had to pray before God would send the rain (1 Kings 18:1, 41-45). God will not carry out His will alone. He has to wait for us to pray before He will carry out His will. What is prayer? It is first for God to have a will, second for us to touch this will and pray for it, and third for God to answer our prayer when we pray.

Many people have the wrong concept that the reason man prays to God is to initiate something and ask God to do something. But the Bible shows us that God first has a will and wants to do something, next He shows us His will, and then we speak out with our mouth the will that we have come to understand. This is prayer. The Lord taught us to pray. God Himself wants His name to be sanctified. God Himself wants His kingdom to come, and God Himself wants His will to be done on earth. Yet God will not do these things alone. He is waiting for the church to pray. If you pray, I pray, and all of God's children pray and if the prayers are numerous enough, His name will be sanctified, His kingdom will come, and His will will be done on earth as it is in heaven. God's children must learn to pray this kind of prayer. We have to always remember what God desires and what He wants to do. Although God has determined to do something, He will not do it; He has to wait for His children to be motivated and willing to express His will through their prayer before He will answer their prayer. Although the ultimate fulfillment of His name being sanctified, His kingdom coming, and His will being done on earth will be in the millennium, the timing of it, whether it will come early or late, depends on the prayer of His children. The basic principle is that God will not do anything according to His purpose alone; He will wait for His children to pray on earth before He does anything.

Some matters can be considered only miscellaneous matters in God's will. But God has a very great will, and the miscellaneous matters of His will are included in this great will. When we pay attention to God's great will, all the miscellaneous matters will be accomplished. God has His will in heaven, and His Spirit conveys this will to us. Therefore, we can echo with the cry, "God, we ask that You accomplish this." When this happens, God accomplishes His will. This is the principle of prayer as revealed in the Bible. God's move today is affected by our prayer on earth. We have to ask God to open our eyes so that we can see that the move in heaven is affected by our prayer on earth. Our Lord has revealed this mystery to us which was hidden from the ages. Brothers and sisters, if we are willing to make a sacrifice and set aside the time to pray, we will see that this kind of prayer will not only receive God's answer but will also receive a reward.

God's will is like a river, and our prayer is like the channel. If our prayer is big, the accomplishment of our prayer will also be big. If our prayer is limited, the accomplishment of our prayer will also be limited. The revival in Wales during 1903-1904 was the greatest revival in the history of the church. God brought in a great revival through a coal miner, Evan Roberts. He did not have much education. But his prayers were profound. Later he did not engage in any public work for seven or eight years. When a brother met him, the brother asked, "What have you been doing all these years?" He answered with one short sentence, "I have been praying the prayer of the kingdom." Brothers and sisters, if there is no prayer, the kingdom will not come. If the channels are blocked, the water cannot flow through. In teaching us to pray, the Lord revealed God's mind and God's demand on us. Whenever God's children place their will in harmony with God's will, God's name will be sanctified, His kingdom will surely come, and His will will indeed be done on earth as in heaven.

THREE THINGS TO PRAY FOR ONESELF

The second section is on three things that one prays for oneself.

The First Thing: "Give Us Today Our Daily Bread"

When some read this, they do not understand why the Lord turns suddenly from God's name, His kingdom, and His will to our daily bread. Is it not a big step backward to turn from such a high prayer to such low matters? Brothers and sisters, there is a reason for this. When a true man of God prays continuously for His name, kingdom, and will, the Lord takes care of the man himself. If the prayer is important, the praying one will surely stir up the attack of Satan. Hence, our bread is one thing that we have to pray for. Bread is man's immediate need. It is also a great temptation. When a man falls into a situation where daily bread becomes a problem, he is in a great trial. On the one hand, we pray that His name be sanctified, His kingdom come, and His will be done on earth. On the other hand, as human beings, we still live on earth; we still need our daily bread. Satan knows this. Consequently, there is a need for protective prayers. This is the prayer of a Christian concerning his own need; he has to ask for the Lord's protection. Otherwise, he may have a lofty prayer on the one hand while coming under attack on the other hand. Satan can attack. When we are short of bread, we are attacked, and our prayer will be affected. We have to see the need of this prayer. We are still human beings on earth, and our body has the need of bread. Therefore, we have to ask God to give us our bread.

This prayer also shows us that we have to look to God and pray to Him every day. The Lord teaches us to pray: "Give us *today* our daily bread." We do not pray weekly, but daily. On earth we have no support, and we have no savings. To some extent we cannot pray for weekly bread or monthly bread; we have to pray for bread *today*. How much trust in God is required here! The Lord is not ignorant of our daily needs; He does not tell us to forget about praying for these needs. Rather, He tells us to pray daily. Actually, the Father already knows the things that we need. The Lord wants us to ask God for our bread day by day because He wants us to learn to look to the Father day by day; He wants us to exercise our faith day by day. We often extend our worries too much into the future, and we stretch our prayer too much into the future. Brothers and sisters, if we have a strong desire to be for His name, His kingdom, and His will, we will suffer great hardships. But if God will give us our daily bread, we will not have to pray for tomorrow's bread until tomorrow comes. Brothers and sisters, do not worry about tomorrow; sufficient for the day is its own evil (Matt. 6:31-34).

The Second Thing: "Forgive Us Our Debts, as We Also Have Forgiven Our Debtors"

On the one hand, there is the demand for our material needs. On the other hand, there is the demand of a good conscience. Day by day, we commit offenses against God. In many things, we may not have sinned, but we have incurred debts. Failing to do what we should do is to incur a debt. Failing to say what we should say is to incur a debt. It is not easy for us to maintain a good conscience before God. Every night when we go to bed, we realize that we have committed many offenses against God. They may not be sins, but they are all debts. We have to ask God to forgive us and forgive our debts before we can have a good conscience. This is very important. To be forgiven of our debts is like being forgiven of our sins; we must have it before we can have a good conscience and before we can live before God with boldness. Many brothers and sisters have the experience that as soon as their conscience has a leakage their faith is gone. We must not have any leakage in our conscience. Concerning faith and a good conscience, Paul said that "some, thrusting these away, have become shipwrecked regarding the faith" (1 Tim. 1:19). The conscience is like a ship; it cannot afford to have any holes. Once the conscience has a hole, faith leaks out. The conscience cannot have any debts; it cannot accumulate any offenses. Once it has any offense, it will have a hole, and the first thing that will leak away is our faith. If the conscience has a hole, one cannot believe even if he tries to. Once condemnation arises in the conscience, faith will leak away. Therefore, brothers and sisters, in order to maintain a good conscience, we have to ask God to forgive our debts. This is a crucial matter. This forgiving of our debt has nothing to do with our receiving of eternal life. But it has to do with our fellowship and with God's discipline.

We have to ask God to forgive our debts as we have forgiven our debtors. If a person is mean toward other brothers and sisters and does not forget their offenses against him, he cannot ask God to forgive his debts. A narrow-minded person, who always pays attention to how others have offended, hurt, or ill-treated him, cannot pray such a prayer before God. A man must have a forgiving heart before he can boldly ask the Father: "Forgive us our debts, as we also have forgiven our debtors." One cannot hold his debtor responsible while asking God to forgive his own debts. If we have not forgiven our debtors, how can we open our mouth to ask God to forgive our debts? Brothers and sisters, if we have not received something from someone, and we harbor a discontent in our heart, calculating the offenses that others have done against us, how can we have this kind of prayer to the Father? Brothers and sisters, just as our offenses before God must be forgiven, so we also must forgive the offenses of others against us. We must first forgive the debts of others before we can pray boldly to the Father: "Forgive us our debts, as we also have forgiven our debtors."

Here we have to pay attention to one thing: The Bible tells us not only about our relationship with the Father but also about our relationship with one another as brothers and sisters. If a brother only remembers his relationship with God and forgets his relationship with other brothers and sisters and presumes that there is nothing wrong between him and God, he is deceiving himself. Brothers and sisters, never overlook your relationship with the brothers and sisters. If there is a barrier between you and another brother or sister, you will immediately lose God's blessing. If there is something which you should do to a brother or a sister or if there is something you should say to them and you have not done it, you may not have sinned, but you have incurred a debt. Do not think that everything is all right just because you have not sinned. You must be without debt also. At the same time, if a brother or sister owes you anything and you do not forget it, you are not forgiving their debts. This will also hinder you from being forgiven by God. God will deal with you in the same way that you deal with the brothers and sisters. If you do not forget their debt and if you keep on counting and complaining, you are being grossly deceived if you think that God has forgiven your debts. The Lord clearly teaches us to pray: "Forgive us our debts, as we also have forgiven our debtors." We have to pay attention to the words "as we also have forgiven." If there were no words "have forgiven," it would be impossible to use the word "as." If we have not forgiven our debtors, our debts will be remembered before God. If we have removed from our heart their debt and there is nothing there anymore, we can come boldly before God and say, "Forgive us our debts, as we also have forgiven our debtors." God will have to forgive us. Brothers and sisters, we must thoroughly forgive our debtors. Otherwise, it will affect our being forgiven before God.

The Third Thing:
"Do Not Bring Us into Temptation, but Deliver Us from the Evil One"

The first part speaks of our material needs. The second part speaks of our relationship with the brothers and sisters. This part speaks of our relationship with Satan. "Do not bring us into temptation." This is the negative request. "But deliver us from the evil one." This is the positive request. On the one hand, when we live for God on earth and have a strong desire to be for His name, His kingdom, and His will, we have material needs; we need to ask for our daily bread. On the other hand, our conscience needs to be clean and void of offense before God; we need God to forgive our debts. But there is another thing. We also need peace; we need to ask God to deliver us from the hands of Satan. Brothers and sisters, the more we take the way of the kingdom of the heavens, the greater the temptations will be. What then should we do? We can pray and ask God not to "bring us into temptation." Brothers and sisters, we cannot be so confident in ourselves that we can scorn any temptation. Since the Lord has asked us to pray, we should pray that God would not bring us into temptation. We do not know when temptation will come. But we can pray ahead of time that we not be brought into temptation. This prayer is for our protection. We are not waiting every day for temptation to come. Rather, we are praying every day for temptation not to come. We should ask that we only encounter what the Lord allows to come upon us and not encounter anything that the Lord does not allow to come upon us. If we do not pray this way, we will not be able to withstand temptation for a moment; we will not be able to accomplish anything. We must ask the Lord to not bring us into any temptation, not allowing us to encounter anyone that we should not encounter nor to come across anything that we should not come across. This is a protective prayer. Brothers and sisters, we have to pray for God to protect us so that our daily bread is provided, our conscience is clean, and we do not face temptation. In everything, we have to ask the Lord not to bring us into temptation. We should pray that we do not encounter anything that the Lord has not permitted. Daily, we have to ask God to keep us from temptation.

Not only do we have to ask God not to bring us into temptation, but we also have to ask Him to "deliver us from the evil one." This is a positive prayer. No matter where Satan puts his hand, we have to ask the Lord to deliver us from the evil one. In our daily bread, in the matter of condemnation in our conscience, and in any temptation, we have to ask the Lord to deliver us from the evil one. In other words, we pray that we not fall into the hand of the evil one in anything. In reading Matthew 8 and 9, we find that Satan's hands are beyond what we expect and know. They are hidden behind the fever which comes suddenly upon a person's body (8:14) and the storm which rises suddenly from the sea (8:24). They cause the demons to attach themselves to men and drown the pigs (8:28-32). They work within man's heart and cause him to reject and oppose the Lord for no reason at all (9:3, 11).

In short, Satan is out to harm man and inflict suffering on man. Therefore, we have to pray that we will be delivered from the evil one.

The three desires concerning God are basic prayers, and the three requests for ourselves are protective prayers. We ask the Lord for our daily bread not only because we want to eat. We ask that our conscience be without offense not only for the sake of having a good conscience. We ask the Lord to deliver us from the evil one not only because we want to be delivered from the harm of the evil one. We pray for all of these things in order to live longer on earth to perform the work of prayer so that the Father's name will be sanctified, His kingdom will come, and His will will be done on earth as in heaven.

THREE THINGS TO GIVE PRAISE FOR

Lastly, the Lord taught us to give praise for three things: "For Yours is the kingdom and the power and the glory forever. Amen." This praise tells us that the kingdom belongs to the Father, the power belongs to the Father, and the glory belongs to the Father. The three things that we give praise for have to do with deliverance from the evil one. They also have to do with the whole prayer that the Lord taught. We pray that the Lord would deliver us from the evil one because the kingdom is the Father's and not Satan's, because the power is the Father's and not Satan's, and because the glory is the Father's and not Satan's. This is the main point: since the kingdom belongs to the Father, we should not fall into the hand of Satan; since the power belongs to the Father, we should not fall into the hand of Satan; and since the glory belongs to the Father, we should not fall into the hand of Satan. This is the strong reason behind not falling into Satan's hand. If we fall into Satan's hand, how can we glorify the Father any longer? If the Father is to have power over us, Satan cannot have power over us. Since the kingdom of the heavens belongs to the Father, we cannot and should not fall into Satan's hand.

Concerning authority, we should remember the Lord's word. He said, "Behold, I have given you the authority to tread upon serpents and scorpions and over all the power of the enemy, and nothing shall by any means hurt you" (Luke 10:19). This verse says that the authority He gives enables us to overcome all the power of the enemy. With authority there is power. The Lord wants us to know that with the kingdom, there is authority, and behind the authority, the power to rule. The kingdom is God's and not Satan's. Authority belongs to God, not to Satan. Consequently, power belongs to God, not to Satan. Of course, glory also belongs to God, not to Satan. Since the kingdom, the power, and the glory all belong to God, those who belong to God should overcome all temptation and be delivered from the hand of Satan.

In the New Testament, the Lord's name denotes authority, while the Holy Spirit denotes power. All authority is in the Lord's name, while all power is in the Holy Spirit. The Holy Spirit is the power of God. The kingdom denotes the rule of heaven and the authority of God, while the power tells us that all power is in the Holy Spirit. When God moves, the Holy Spirit becomes His power. Since the kingdom belongs to God, Satan has nowhere to exercise his reign. Since the power belongs to the Holy Spirit, Satan can in no way touch the Holy Spirit. Matthew 12:28 tells us that whenever the demons touched the Holy Spirit, they were cast out. Finally, glory also belongs to God. Hence, we can declare and loudly give praise: "For Yours is the kingdom and the power and the glory forever. Amen."

The Lord taught us to pray in this way. This does not mean that we should recite it as a ritualistic ceremony, but pray according to this pattern. All prayers should be according to this pattern. Concerning God, we desire that His name be sanctified, His kingdom come, and His will be done on earth as in heaven. Concerning ourselves, we ask that God would protect us. Concerning our praise, it is based on the fact that the kingdom, the power, and the glory are His. Since the kingdom, the power, and the glory are His, His name should be sanctified, His kingdom should come, and His will should be done on earth as in heaven. Since the kingdom, the power, and the glory are His, we pray to Him concerning our daily bread, our debt, our temptation, and the evil one. Every prayer should take this prayer as its pattern. Some have said that this prayer is not for Christians because it does not end with the words "in the name of the Lord." This is foolish. The prayer that the Lord teaches is not an incantation that we pray. What prayer in the New Testament ends with the words "in the name of the Lord"? When the disciples were on the boat, and they cried, "Lord, save us; we are perishing" (Matt. 8:25), did they end with the words "in the name of the Lord"? The Lord did not teach us to say these words. He taught us to pray according to this principle. He taught us the way to pray. He did not tell us to pray with these words.

THE IMPORTANCE OF FORGIVING OTHERS' OFFENSES

After the Lord finished His teaching on prayer, He went on to say, "For if you forgive men their offenses, your heavenly Father will forgive you also; but if you do not forgive men their offenses, neither will your Father forgive your offenses." This is the Lord's interpretation of verse 12, which says, "Forgive us our debts, as we also have forgiven our debtors." It is easy for Christians to fail in the matter of forgiving others. If any unforgivingness exists among God's children, all lessons, faith, and power will leak away. This is why the Lord is so strong and clear. This is a simple word. Yet God's children need this simple word. "For if you forgive men their offenses, your heavenly Father will forgive you also." It is so simple for us to receive the Father's forgiveness. However, "if you do not forgive men their offenses, neither will your Father forgive your offenses." There is no such thing as careless forgiveness. This word is simple, but the fact is not that simple. If we forgive others with our mouth but do not forgive in our heart, it is not considered as forgiveness in the Father's eyes. Forgiveness which is in the mouth only is vain and deceitful and does not count before the Father. We must forgive others' offenses from the heart. Just as the disciples needed this word of the Lord, we also need the same word. If Christians are irreconcilable and if they do not forgive others from their heart, the church will run into problems. If we have no intention of behaving like the church and if we want to each take our own way as soon as we disagree with a single word, we do not need to forgive one another. But the Lord knows how crucial this matter is to us. Therefore, He reemphasized it at the end of the prayer. The Lord knows that the more we communicate and fellowship with one another, the more we need to forgive one another. He knows how crucial this matter is. Therefore, He had to turn our attention to it. If we do not forgive one another, it will be easy for us to give place to the devil. If we cannot forgive one another, we are not people of the kingdom, and we cannot do the work of the kingdom. No one who is unforgiving can be in the work of the kingdom, and no one who is unforgiving can be a person in the kingdom. Whenever we develop a problem with the brothers and sisters, we develop a problem with the Lord. We cannot pray to the Lord on the one hand and remain unforgiving on the other hand. Brothers and sisters, this is not an insignificant thing. We must pay attention to what the Lord pays attention to. We must forgive others their offenses.

Finally, we should note how much the Lord cares for the matter of prayer. There are only four verses that speak about almsgiving. In speaking about fasting, there are only three verses. But concerning prayer, He speaks in an emphatic way because prayer has to do with God. Prayer is the most important work of a Christian. The Lord shows us that there is reward for prayer because prayer is too great an issue; it is too great a matter. Those who are faithful to this work of prayer will receive a reward. Those who continue with this work in secret and who pay attention to this work will not be without reward. May God raise up those who would pray for God's work.

Moreover, the prayer that the Lord taught always mentions "we" and "us." This is the form of address used by the church. This is a prayer that is filled with a sense of the Body. It is a tremendous prayer. I do not know how many saints there are on earth who can pray this prayer. Brothers and sisters, may we consecrate ourselves afresh for this great prayer. Countless saints throughout the ages have become a part of this great prayer. May the Lord be merciful to us that we also may have a share in this great prayer.

CHAPTER THREE

IN THE NAME OF THE LORD JESUS—
GOD'S COMMITMENT

Scripture Reading: Phil. 2:9-11; Eph. 1:21; John 14:13-14; 15:16; 16:23-24, 26a; Mark 16:17; Luke 10:17-19; 24:47; Acts 3:6; 4:7, 10, 12; 10:43; 16:18; 19:5; 1 Cor. 6:11

Before God we have to be particularly clear about one thing: the name of the Lord Jesus. No one on earth can be saved without the name of the Lord Jesus, and no one can be useful in the hand of God without knowing the name of the Lord Jesus. We must know the meaning of the name of the Lord Jesus. What a pity that the name of the Lord has become so common in man's conversation! Many times, the phrase *in the name of the Lord Jesus* has become something meaningless! Man often hears and reads this expression repeatedly to the point that he does not know what it means to be in the name of Jesus Christ. We have to ask God to help us understand afresh the significance of the familiar name of the Lord Jesus.

The name of the Lord Jesus is something special. It is something that the Lord did not have while He was on earth. Matthew 1 tells us that when the Lord Jesus was on earth, His name was Jesus. But Philippians 2 says that He became obedient even unto death and that the death of a cross, and therefore, God highly exalted Him and bestowed on Him the name which is above every name. What is this name? Philippians 2:10-11 says, "That in the name of Jesus every knee should bow, of those who are in heaven and on earth and under the earth, and every tongue should openly confess that Jesus Christ is Lord to the glory of God the Father." This name is "the name of Jesus." He did not receive this name when He was on earth. After He ascended to heaven

He received this name. He was already called Jesus when He was on earth. Through His obedience unto death on the cross, God exalted Him. In His exaltation, the name which is above every name was bestowed upon Him. The name which is above every name is "the name of Jesus."

Not only did Paul receive the revelation of such a change in the Lord's name, but also the Lord Jesus Himself spoke of a great change in His own name in the Gospel of John. He said, "Until now you have asked for nothing in My name; ask and you shall receive....In that day you will ask in My name" (John 16:24, 26). "In that day" we will ask in His name. On the day the Lord spoke this word, He had not yet received the name which is above every name. It was not until that day that He received the name above every name. It was not until that day that we could ask the Father in His name.

May the Lord open our eyes to see the great change in the Lord's name after His ascension. We cannot fathom this change in our mind. This name is the name given by God, and it is a name that is above every name.

What does this name signify? This name signifies authority and power. Why does this name signify authority and power? Philippians 2:10-11 says, "That in the name of Jesus every knee should bow, of those who are in heaven and on earth and under the earth, and every tongue should openly confess that Jesus Christ is Lord to the glory of God the Father." This is authority. Every knee has to bow to the name of Jesus, and everyone has to call Jesus the Lord because of His name. Hence, the name of Jesus denotes the fact that God has given Him the all-transcending authority and power.

In Luke 10:17 the disciples said to the Lord, "Lord, even the demons are subject to us in Your name." It was a great thing for the disciples to cast out demons in the name of the Lord. The demons may not be afraid of many names on earth. But when the disciples did anything in the name of the Lord Jesus, the demons were subject to them. Later the Lord explained why His name made the demons subject to them. He said, "I have given you the authority to tread...over all the power of the enemy" (v. 19). Hence, the name equals authority. Where the name is, there is authority.

This is not all. Even the rulers among the Jews knew this. After Peter raised the lame man, the rulers called the apostles before them the next day and asked, "By what power or in what name did you do this?" (Acts 4:7). In other words, what authority did they have in telling the man to stand up and walk? They knew that with every name there was authority. Hence, the name of Jesus denotes all the authority that God has committed to Him. We are not saying that the name itself is the authority; the effect of the name is authority.

In the New Testament, not only do we see the name of Jesus; we also see one very peculiar expression: "in the name of Jesus." Brothers and sisters, have we seen this? It is not just a matter of the name of Jesus Christ but a matter of being in the name of Jesus Christ. If we read God's Word carefully and if we pursue the spiritual pathway, we may often say that we do things in the name of the Lord Jesus or that we do things in the name of Jesus Christ, but actually we do not know what it is to be in this name. If we do not know how to do things in the name of the Lord Jesus, we cannot even be a Christian. Hence, we have to see the meaning of being in the name of the Lord Jesus.

The first time the Lord Jesus mentioned being in His name was in John 14—16. After the Lord washed the disciples' feet, He spoke with the disciples. The Lord said distinctly in these three chapters what we can do when we do things in His name. He said, "Whatever you ask in My name, that I will do....If you ask Me anything in My name, I will do it" (14:13-14). All the way from chapters fourteen through sixteen, He repeatedly told the disciples to ask "in My name." This shows us not only that He would one day receive a name above every name, but also that the disciples could use this name. It is also a name you and I can use. This name is the name God gave to His Son Jesus, which has, in turn, been put in our hands. It is now in my hands and in your hands. You and I and everyone else can now use this name. Consequently, the Bible mentions not only that the Lord Jesus has received a name which is above every name, but it mentions also the experience of being in the name of Jesus Christ. Not only is there His name, but there is also such a thing as being in His name. The name of Jesus Christ is the name He received before God, and being in the name of Jesus Christ is for God's children to partake of this name. Hence, being in the name of the Lord Jesus is to partake of His name. It means that we can use this name. Brothers and sisters, we have to realize that this is the greatest thing committed to us from God and the Lord Jesus.

Why do we say that God has committed the name of Jesus to us? What does *committed* mean? God commissions us to preach the gospel; He commissions us to do a certain work, and He commissions us to go to a certain place and speak for Him. All these are what God has commissioned us to do. But the meaning of being in the name of the Lord Jesus does not refer to this kind of commission. Being in the name of the Lord Jesus means that God has committed His Son to us. God is not committing us to do a work; He has committed His Son to us. God is not charging us to go; He is charging us to take His Son with us. This is the meaning of being in the name of the Lord Jesus.

Being in the name of the Lord Jesus is for God to commit His Son to us. Suppose you have a sum of money in the bank. When you want to withdraw the money, you must use your seal. If you ask a friend to withdraw the money on your behalf, you have to give him the seal. When he goes to withdraw the money, it will be very easy because he has the seal in his hand. When he goes to the bank, writes ten dollars on a check, and puts the seal on the check, he will receive ten dollars. Being in the name of the Lord is like the Lord Jesus giving us His seal. Brothers and sisters, we have a limited amount on deposit, and there is a limit to the amount we can withdraw. But having the seal of the Lord Jesus is a tremendous matter. If I have a large sum of money in the bank and commit the checkbook and seal to someone, I must be prepared to trust in him fully. If I cannot trust him, I will wonder whether he uses my seal to withdraw money. How do I know that he will not write checks with my seal? How do I know that he will not sign contracts with my seal? If I do not trust in a person, I cannot commit my seal to his hand. If I give him my seal, it means that I acknowledge everything he does. This is what it means to be in the name of the Lord Jesus. It means that the Lord is bold enough to commit His name to our hand, and He is allowing us to use this name. The Lord trusts us to the extent that He dares to commit His name to our hands and allow us to use this name. This is the meaning of being in the name of the Lord Jesus. Being in the name of the Lord means that the Lord Jesus has given Himself to us and that He is willing to acknowledge everything that we do in His name. He is willing to bear all the consequences of us doing things in His name.

Sometimes we tell someone, "Go and tell a certain brother what to do. If he asks you who said it, just tell him that I said it." This is being in the name of someone. Being in someone's name is to use that name. If you commit your name to someone and he uses your name, you have to bear the responsibility of his use of your name. This is what it means by being in the name.

The last night the Lord Jesus was on earth, He told the disciples, "Whatever you ask in My name, that I will do, that the Father may be glorified in the Son. If you ask Me anything in My name, I will do it" (John 14:13-14). This means that the Lord Jesus committed a great thing to the disciples; He gave the disciples His name. His name is authority, and there is nothing that He can give that is greater than this. Suppose that after the Lord Jesus committed His name to our hand, we used it irresponsibly. What would happen? A man who occupies an important position needs only to put his seal to his order, and the order is executed. If he gives his seal to someone, he will have to be responsible every time the seal is used to issue an order. Do you think he can commit his seal to anyone easily? Of course he cannot. But the Lord Jesus has committed His name to us. The Lord's name is a name that is above every name. He is willing to commit this name to you and me and allow us to use this name. Do we see the responsibility in committing His name to us? God trusts us and commits the Lord Jesus' name to us. Whatever we do in His name, God will take responsibility for it. Brothers and sisters, what a tremendous thing this is! God will take responsibility for whatever we do in the name of the Lord Jesus!

One characteristic of this age is that the Lord Jesus does not do anything directly. He does not speak directly on earth; rather, He speaks through the church. He does not perform any miracles directly; rather, He performs them through the church. He does not save men directly; rather, He saves them through the church. Today the Lord accomplishes His work through the church rather than directly by Himself. This is why He has committed His name to the church. But what a great responsibility He has to bear. It is easy to take responsibility for what you do directly. All you have to do is be responsible for what you do personally; you do not have to take responsibility for what others do. If your seal is in your hand, you will take responsibility only for what you do yourself. But if your seal is in someone else's hand, you will have to be responsible for what they do with your seal. If the Lord Jesus was in the world today, working the same way as He did before by doing everything Himself, He would not have to take responsibility for what we do. But today the Lord's work is not done by Himself alone. He has committed His work to the church. All the works of the Lord Jesus today are in the church. Today the church's work is the Lord's work. Hence, He has to take responsibility for everything the church does with His name. In committing a task to someone, we have to find a reliable person. If a person is not reliable, it is hard to commit anything to him. But today the Lord Jesus is obligated to commit Himself to the church. Now is not the time for the Son of God to appear in the flesh. Now is the time when the Son of God appears in the Spirit and in the church. Since this is so, He has to commit Himself to the church. Otherwise, He could not do anything. Today He has ascended to the heavens and is sitting on the right hand of the Father, waiting for the enemy to be His footstool. He is there as the High Priest, and He is praying there. This is His job. As to His work on earth, He has committed it to the church. Therefore, the church has the authority to use His name today. Consequently, the Lord has to take responsibility for the church's use of His name.

On earth the church has no greater authority than the authority of doing things in the Lord Jesus' name. The Lord has committed His name to the church. This is the greatest commitment because this name denotes Himself. Whatever you speak in the name of the Lord Jesus becomes what the Lord Himself speaks. Whatever you ask in the name of the Lord Jesus becomes what He asks. Whatever you decide in the name of the Lord Jesus becomes what the Lord decides. The church has the authority to speak in the name of the Lord. What a commitment God has given to the church!

We see in the Bible one example of acting in the name of the Lord. When the archangel Michael argued with the devil over the body of Moses, did he say, "I rebuke you" or "May the Lord rebuke you"? If you add the word *may,* it becomes a prayer and a wish. No, the archangel said, "The Lord rebuke you"! (Jude 9). This means that for him to rebuke the devil is for the Lord to rebuke him. The archangel Michael applied the Lord's name. Hence, being in the name of the Lord Jesus does not necessarily mean saying the words "in the name of the Lord Jesus." Doing things in the name of the Lord Jesus means that we use His name as we use our own name. Here we touch a very important spiritual principle: we can use the Lord's name as we use our own name. Many people say that they have not exhausted the power in the Lord's blood. I would say rather that we have not exhausted the power in His name. Paul could say to the Corinthians, "I have no commandment of the Lord, but I give my opinion." Further on, he said, "I think that I also have the Spirit of God" (1 Cor. 7:25, 40). We have to see that this name is a name that we can use. Brothers and sisters, do you realize that here is a name, an authority, and a power that have been placed in the hand of the church? The church can use them. The church should use the Lord's name in a proper way. We say that the church reigns. But without the name, there would be no way that the church could reign. We say that the church holds the key to the kingdom and is responsible for bringing in the kingdom. But without the name, the gate of the kingdom could not be opened. We say that God's intention is for the church to bind up death through life and bind up Satan. Yet if we did not have this name or did not know how to use this name, there would be no way for us to accomplish these things. We have to see that the Lord Jesus has given this name to the church.

This is why God charges that a man must be baptized after he has believed in the Lord and is saved. What is baptism? It is coming into the Lord's name. On the day I was baptized, I began to share this name. From that day on, God committed this name to me. I can use the Lord Jesus' name as I use my own name. This is why baptism is such a great matter. According to the spiritual reality, I am a dead man and I am also a resurrected man. Since I am standing on the ground of death and resurrection, I can use the Lord's name. From that day, I became related to His name. He is Christ, and we are the Christians. What is a Christian? What is the church? The church is just a group of people on earth who can use the Lord's name, and God takes responsibility for their action every time they use that name. In whatever way we use this name, God will take responsibility for it. This is a tremendous thing. Our relationship with the Lord's name began at the time of baptism. We are baptized into the name. In other words, through baptism we enter into the name.

Here we see that the cross and resurrection are two indispensable things. Only by standing on the ground of baptism can we use the Lord's name. If we are not standing on the ground of baptism, we cannot use His name, because the cross will not have a free way in us, and the Lord Jesus will not have any effect on us; we cannot use the name. Even if we use the name, God will not take responsibility for it. We must stand on the ground of baptism. The ground of baptism means that we believe in the fact of the cross and believe that the old man is crucified with Christ; we accept the principle of the cross and receive the cross as something that deals with our natural life. Baptism tells us that everything we have must go through death daily. Only that which remains after passing through death has spiritual significance. If something is gone after it passes through death, it will not stand before God. God wants the things that pass through the cross and remain, the things that are not destroyed after death has done its work.

God's children need to see the fact of the cross. We need God to reveal what we have received in Christ. The day must come when the Lord breaks the backbone of our natural life. Only then will we become useful. The day must come when God sees the mark of the cross in us. In many people, it does not seem as if the cross has done any work. It does not seem as if the cross has done any work in their speech, in the way they work, in their feeling, and particularly in their attitude before God. The day must come when God breaks and destroys such a person by the cross. Only that which remains after the cross is resurrection. Resurrection is that which is not terminated through death; it is that which is not annihilated through death. Resurrection is what remains after a person is smitten by the Lord. Only those who stand on such a ground can exercise the Lord's authority, and only they can use the Lord's name. God assumes responsibility for those who stand on this ground, and He is behind them when they use the Lord's name. Brothers and sisters, this is the greatest commitment in the whole world. God can commit His Son's name to us and allow us to use this name as our own. This is too great a matter. God has to assume tremendous responsibility in this matter. This is, indeed, not a small matter.

When we do things in the Lord's name, what result will this name bring? The Bible shows us that there are three results of acting in the Lord's name. The first relates to man, the second to the devil, and the third to God.

THE EFFECT ON MAN

Luke 24:47 says, "And that repentance for forgiveness of sins would be proclaimed in His name to all the nations, beginning from Jerusalem." Acts 10:43 says, "To this One all the prophets testify that through His name everyone who believes into Him will receive forgiveness of sins." First Corinthians 6:11 says, "And these things were some of you; but you were washed, but you were sanctified, but you were justified in the name of the Lord Jesus Christ and in the

Spirit of our God." The clearest passage concerning this matter is in Acts 3:2-6, "And a certain man who had been lame from his mother's womb was being carried there, whom they had laid day by day at the door of the temple which is called Beautiful to ask alms from those entering into the temple. And he, seeing Peter and John about to go into the temple, began to ask to receive alms. And Peter, gazing at him with John, said, Look at us! And he turned his attention to them, expecting to receive something from them. But Peter said, Silver and gold I do not possess, but what I have, this I give to you: In the name of Jesus Christ the Nazarene rise up and walk." Brothers and sisters, do you know what it is to speak to others in the name of Jesus Christ the Nazarene? If you were not standing on the ground of death, resurrection, and baptism, what would you do? You would probably kneel down and pray, "Lord, I do not know if this lame man should be healed. Show us if this lame man should be healed. If he should be healed, please make us clear, and please give us the boldness. If he should not be healed, we will just let the matter go." This was not the apostles' experience. The apostles did not feel that the Lord's name remained with the Lord and that they had to ask for permission to do anything. The apostles realized that the name of Jesus the Nazarene was theirs; they owned it, and they could use it.

What is the church? The church is a group of people on earth who maintain the Lord's name. God has called men out of the nations into His name. This is the church. The church maintains the Lord's name on earth. This is why the church can use the Lord's name and apply it to people. We can say to others, "Rise up and be baptized and wash away your sins, calling on His name" (Acts 22:16). When the Lord Jesus was on earth, He said to a woman, "Daughter, your faith has healed you. Go in peace" (Luke 8:48). Another time He told a paralytic, "Take courage, child; your sins are forgiven" (Matt. 9:2). Brothers and sisters, if we are standing on the ground of baptism and we have the vision and revelation, we will realize that we are in charge of the Lord's name. When we preach the gospel to someone and they receive it, to some extent we can say, "Brother, go home. The Lord Jesus has forgiven you." We do not have to wait for him to say anything; we can pronounce him saved.

Because of the healing of the lame man, the rulers, elders, and scribes called the apostles to their midst and asked, "By what power or in what name did you do this?" (Acts 4:7). At that time, Peter was filled with the Holy Spirit, and he said to them, "Let it be known to you all and to all the people of Israel that in the name of Jesus Christ the Nazarene, whom you crucified and whom God has raised from the dead, in this name this man stands before you in good health." After he said this, he declared, "And there is salvation in no other, for neither is there another name under heaven given among men in which we must be saved" (Acts 4:10, 12). Only this name, this unique name, can save us. We can use this name and apply it to men.

THE EFFECT ON THE DEVIL

We can apply this name not only to man but also to the devil. Mark 16:17 says, "In My name they will cast out demons." How do we cast out demons in His name? Acts 16 records Paul meeting a slave girl possessed by a spirit. For many days, she bothered Paul. The Bible says, "Paul was greatly disturbed." He was disturbed by her. What did he do? He did not pray, and he did not do many other things. He just turned around and said to the spirit, "I charge you in the name of Jesus Christ to come out of her" (v. 18). Just one word of command and the spirit departed from her. The name of the Lord Jesus was committed to Paul, and he used this name. We have to realize that when the Lord's name is committed to us, it is no longer kept in heaven. If our spiritual condition is normal, His name will be in our hand. When Paul was disturbed, he charged the spirit to come out. He did not pray to the Lord. We may think that he was not spiritual, that he acted independently, and that he had not sought God's will. But when Paul rebuked the spirit, the spirit left. The real issue is whether or not we are living before God and whether we are standing on the proper ground. If we are standing on the right ground, we will see that the Lord's name is in our hand. Being in the Lord's name is not an empty word. The Lord's name is a name that we can use. We can use this name to work and to cast out demons.

In Luke 10 the Lord sent the disciples out. The Lord had not yet ascended, but He was acting from the position of ascension. Hence, He said, "I was watching Satan fall like lightning out of heaven" (v. 18). When the disciples went out, the Lord Jesus did not go with them. Yet they took the Lord's name with them. Later the disciples came back and reported to the Lord, "Even the demons are subject to us in Your name" (v. 17). Why were they subject to the disciples? It is because the disciples did it "...in Your name." They held the Lord's name in their hands, and authority was in their hands. Therefore, the Lord Jesus said, "I have given you the authority to tread upon serpents and scorpions and over all the power of the enemy" (v. 19). Brothers and sisters, have we seen this? With the Lord's name, we can deal with all the power of the enemy. God has to open our eyes to see that He has given us the name of the Lord Jesus. This is God's commitment to us.

THE EFFECT TOWARD GOD

Moreover, the Lord's name has been given to us not only to deal with men, to save men, to heal men, to have authority over the demons, and to cast them out of men. Even more precious is the fact that the Lord's name enables us to go to the Father and speak to Him. When we go to the Father in this way, He has to answer us. John 14—16 speaks of the Lord's name three times. We have to say with reverence that the Lord Jesus was very bold! What did He say? "And whatever you ask in My name, that I will do, that the Father may be glorified in the Son. If you ask Me anything in My name, I will do it" (14:13-14). Oh, this name is above all other names! This name is the name every tongue in heaven, on earth, and under the earth should openly confess as Lord. It is the name to which every knee should bow! This name is powerful before God; God honors this name. When we do things in this name, God honors it. The Lord said, "You did not choose Me, but I chose you, and I set you that you should go forth and bear fruit and that your fruit should remain, that whatever you ask the Father in My name, He may give you" (15:16). Again He said, "And in that day you will ask Me nothing. Truly, truly, I say to you, Whatever you ask the Father in My name, He will give to you. Until now you have asked for nothing in My name; ask and you shall receive, that your joy may be made full" (16:23-24). Brothers and sisters, can we think of another promise greater than this?

What then is praying in the name of the Lord Jesus? Praying in the name of the Lord Jesus is saying to God, "I am not trustworthy. I am useless. But I am praying in the name of Jesus." Suppose you send a letter to a friend through a messenger, asking your friend to return a sum of money through the same messenger. When your friend sees the signature, he should give the money to the messenger. Is this not right? Will your friend ask the messenger, "Are you educated? What is your family background? Who is in your family? How is your temper?" He will surely not ask these questions. He is not concerned with who the messenger is. He only needs to make sure that the letter has your signature. The messenger has come in your name, and you have put your trust in this messenger. Hallelujah! To stand before God in the name of the Lord Jesus is to say that you do not stand on your own merit but on the merit of the Lord's name. It is to say that you are not counting on what you are or what you will be, but on what the name of the Lord is. Many people pray with the hope that they will be answered in the future. Some pray with the hope that they will be answered in a few months or a few years. They hope in this way because they expect to become better in a few years. Because they expect to become better, they expect that their prayer will be answered. But we have to realize that our prayer is answered because of His name and not because of our name. We have to completely deny our flesh, and we need to be in the name of the Lord Jesus. All the ground we have is gained through Him. We stand before God because of Him and not because of ourselves. It is not because of our righteousness but because of His blood; it is not based on what we want but on what He wants. We are here in the name of the Lord.

Brothers and sisters, the knowledge of the name of the

Lord Jesus is a revelation and not a doctrine. The day will come when God opens our eyes to see the power in this name, the greatness in this name, and what a wonder it is that God has committed this name to us. Because God has committed His Son's name to us, we can say, "God, we do this in the name of Your Son Jesus." This means, "God, You believe in us. You trust in us. You take responsibility for everything that we do." Brothers and sisters, since this name is placed in our hands for the purpose of dealing with men, the devil, and God, we should realize that we must live a certain kind of life before we can have the power to use this name. Therefore, we must learn to know the cross every day. Only then can we apply this name. Brothers and sisters, please remember that the cross cannot be separated from this name. May the cross work deeply in us to the extent that we know how to apply this name to men, how to use this name to deal with the devil, and how to pray to the Father through this name. May the Lord give the church abundant knowledge concerning this name so that the position, authority, and power of this name is recovered among us today and the church will receive many spiritual riches through His name.

CHAPTER FOUR

THE PRAYER OF AUTHORITY

Scripture Reading: Matt. 18:18-19; Mark 11:23-24; Eph. 1:20-22; 2:6; 6:12-13, 18-19

The Bible contains a most lofty and spiritual prayer. But few people pray this prayer, and few pay attention to it. What is this prayer? It is the "prayer of authority." We know that there are prayers of praise, prayers of thanksgiving, supplicating prayers, and begging prayers. But few of us know that there is a prayer of authority. A prayer of authority is a commanding prayer. This is the most crucial and most spiritual prayer in the Bible. This kind of prayer is a sign of authority and a declaration of authority.

Brothers and sisters, if you want to be a man of prayer, you have to learn to pray with authority. This kind of prayer is described by the Lord in Matthew 18:18. "Whatever you bind on the earth shall have been bound in heaven, and whatever you loose on the earth shall have been loosed in heaven." In this verse, there is a prayer that is called a binding prayer and a prayer that is called a loosing prayer. The move in heaven is dependent on the move on earth. Heaven listens to the earth and obeys the command of the earth. Whatever the earth binds will be bound in heaven, and whatever the earth looses will be loosed in heaven. The earth does not pray; it binds and looses. This is to pray with authority.

Isaiah 45:11 has the phrase, "Command Me." How can we command God? This appears too presumptuous. But this is God's own word. We cannot give excuse to the flesh, but this shows us a commanding prayer, a prayer in the form of an order. As far as God is concerned, we can order Him, and we can command Him. Everyone who endeavors to learn to pray must learn this kind of prayer.

We can consider the story in Exodus 14. When Moses brought the Israelites out of Egypt to the Red Sea, trouble arose. Before them was the Red Sea, and behind them were the armies of the Egyptians. They were caught between two perils. When the Israelites saw the Egyptians approaching, they were afraid. On the one hand, they implored the Lord. On the other hand, they murmured against Moses. What did Moses do? From God's answer, we know that Moses was pleading. God said to Moses, "Wherefore criest thou unto me? speak unto the children of Israel, that they go forward: but lift thou up thy rod, and stretch out thine hand over the sea, and divide it: and the children of Israel shall go on dry ground through the midst of the sea" (vv. 15-16). The rod which God gave Moses was a symbol of His authority. He was telling Moses that he could pray with authority; there was no need to cry out to Him. Once there was the commanding prayer, He would carry out the work. Moses was learning, and he eventually learned, to pray with authority, that is, to pray the commanding prayer.

At what point did this kind of commanding prayer begin for Christians?

This kind of prayer began from the time the Lord ascended to the heavenlies. Ascension is very much related to our Christian life. How are these two things related? Ascension makes us victorious. The death of Christ dealt with the old creation in Adam, while resurrection brought us into the new creation. Ascension secured a new position for us before Satan; it is not a new position before God. A new position before God was secured through the Lord's resurrection, while a new position before Satan was secured through the Lord's ascension. Ephesians 1:20-22 says that when Christ ascended, God caused Him to sit at His right hand and made Him "far above all rule and authority and power and lordship and every name that is named not only in this age but also in that which is to come." Furthermore, God "subjected all things under His feet." When Christ ascended, He opened up a way through "the air" to the heavenlies. From that day on, His

church has been able to go from the earth to the heavenlies.
We know that spiritual enemies dwell in "the air." But today
Christ has ascended to the heavenlies. A way from the earth
to the heavenlies is now opened. This way was originally
blocked by Satan. Now Christ has opened up a way to the
heavenlies and has transcended far above all rule and
authority and power and lordship and every name that is
named not only in this age but also in that which is to come.
This is Christ's position today. In other words, God has put
Satan and his subjects under Christ's feet; all things are
under His feet.

There is a difference between the meaning of ascension
and the meaning of death and resurrection. Death and
resurrection are for redemption, while ascension is for
warfare; it is to execute what death and resurrection have
accomplished. Ascension makes it possible to manifest the
new position. Thank the Lord that Ephesians 2:6 tells us that
God has "raised us up together with Him and seated us
together with Him in the heavenlies in Christ Jesus." Brothers
and sisters, have we seen what God has done for us? In
chapter one Christ ascended to be far above all rule and
authority and power and lordship and every name that is
named not only in this age but also in that which is to come.
In chapter two we are seated with Him in the heavenlies.
This means that the church also has transcended far above
all rule and authority and power and lordship and every name
that is named not only in this age but also in that which is
to come. Thank God that this is a fact. Just as Christ
transcended over all things, the church has also transcended
over all things. Just as the Lord transcended over all spiritual
enemies, the church has also transcended over all spiritual
enemies. Just as all spiritual enemies have been overcome by
the ascension of the Lord, the church has also overcome them
by being joined to Christ in His ascension. Hence, all the
spiritual enemies are under the feet of the church.

We have to pay attention to Ephesians 1, 2, and 6. Chapter
one shows us the position of Christ. Chapter two shows us
the church's position in Christ. Chapter six shows us what
the church should do after it has acquired its position in

Christ. Chapter one is on Christ in the heavenlies. Chapter two is on the church being in the heavenlies together with Christ. Chapter six is on spiritual warfare. God has made the church sit together with Christ in the heavenlies. But the church does not sit there forever; God also causes it to stand. Hence, chapter two mentions sitting, while chapter six mentions standing; we stand in our position in the heavenlies. "For our wrestling is...against the rulers, against the authorities, against the world-rulers of this darkness, against the spiritual forces of evil in the heavenlies....and having done all, to stand" (Eph. 6:12-13). Our warfare is against the demons. Hence, it is a spiritual warfare.

Ephesians 6:18-19 says, "By means of all prayer and petition, praying at every time in spirit and watching unto this in all perseverance and petition concerning all the saints, and for me." This is a prayer concerning spiritual warfare. This kind of prayer is different from ordinary prayer. Ordinary prayer is directed from earth to heaven. But the prayer here is not from earth to heaven; it begins from a heavenly position and goes from heaven to earth. A prayer with authority has heaven as its starting point and the earth as its destination. In other words, a prayer with authority is prayed from heaven to earth. Everyone who knows how to pray knows what it is to pray upward and what it is to pray downward. If a man has never learned the prayer that prays downward, he has never learned to pray with authority. In the spiritual warfare, the kind of prayer that prays downward is very important. What is a prayer that prays downward? It is to stand in the position that Christ has given us in the heavenlies, to command Satan with authority and reject all his works, and to proclaim with authority that all God's commands should be accomplished. If we pray for a realization of God's will and a decision concerning it, we should not say, "God, I ask You to accomplish this." Rather, we should say, "God, You have to do this. You have to accomplish this. No matter what happens, You must fulfill this work." This is a commanding prayer, a prayer with authority.

The meaning of the word *amen* is not "so be it" or "may it be so," but "it will be so" and "it will surely come to pass."

When you pray and I say amen, I am saying that things will turn out according to the way you pray. Events must transpire this way, and your prayer will be answered. This is a commanding prayer, a prayer of command that issues from faith. We can say this because we have a heavenly standing. We were brought to our heavenly standing when Christ ascended to the heavenlies. As soon as Christ ascended to the heavenlies, we were there also. This is like saying that as soon as Christ died and resurrected, we died and resurrected. Brothers and sisters, we must see the heavenly position of the church. Satan begins his work by trying to take away our position in the heavenlies. The heavenly position is a position of victory. As long as we stand in that position, we have victory. If Satan succeeds in dragging us down from the heavenlies, we will be defeated. Victory is standing continuously in the heavenly position of victory. Satan will tell us that we are on earth. If we agree with him that we are on earth, we will be defeated. Satan will try to frustrate us by our defeat and make us think that we are indeed on earth. But if we stand up and declare, "Christ is in the heavenlies, and we are also in the heavenlies," and hold on to our position in the heavenlies, we will overcome. Hence, it is a big thing to stand in the right position.

A prayer with authority has the position of being in the heavenlies as its basis. Since the church is in the heavenlies with Christ, it can pray with authority.

What is praying with authority? Simply put, it is praying the prayer of Mark 11. In order to be clear about this truth, we should consider verses 23-24 carefully. Verse 24 begins with the words "for this reason." "For this reason" means that this sentence is a continuation of what has gone before. This means that verse 24 is joined to verse 23. Verse 24 mentions prayer. This proves that verse 23 must also concern prayer. The strange thing is that verse 23 does not sound like an ordinary prayer. The Lord did not tell us to pray, "God, please move the mountain and cast it into the sea." What does it say? It says, "Whoever says to this mountain, Be taken up and cast into the sea." According to our concept, what should a prayer be like? We think that when we pray to God, we have to say, "God, please move this mountain and cast it into the sea." But the Lord said something else. He did not tell us to speak to God; He told us to turn to the mountain and to speak to the mountain. The speaking is not toward God but directly toward the mountain, telling it to be cast into the sea. Since the Lord was afraid that we would not consider this to be a prayer, He pointed out in the following verse that it is a prayer. This prayer is not directed toward God, but it is a prayer. It is a speaking directed toward the mountain that says, "Be taken up and cast into the sea." Yet this is also a prayer. This is a prayer with authority. A prayer with authority does not ask God to do something. Rather, it exercises God's authority and applies this authority to deal with problems and things that ought to be removed. Every overcomer has to learn to pray this kind of prayer. Every overcomer has to learn to speak to the mountain.

We have many weaknesses, such as temper, evil thoughts, or physical illnesses. If we plead with God concerning these problems, it seems that there is not much result. However, if we apply God's authority to the situation and speak to the mountain, these problems will go away. What is the meaning of the word "mountain" in this verse? A mountain is a problem that stands in front of us. A mountain is something that blocks the way and stops us from going on. If we see a mountain, what do we do? When many people encounter a mountain in their life or in their work, they pray to God to remove the mountain. But God tells us to speak to the mountain ourselves. All we have to do is issue a word of command to the mountain: "Be taken up and cast into the sea." There is a great difference between asking God to remove the mountain and commanding the mountain to be removed. It is one thing to go to God and ask Him to do something. It is another thing to directly command the mountain to be cast away. We often overlook this kind of commanding prayer. Seldom do we pray by applying God's authority to the problem or by saying, "I command you in the name of my Lord to go away" or "I cannot tolerate this thing to remain with me anymore." A prayer with authority is one in which we tell the things that are frustrating us to go away. We can say to our temper, "Go away." We can say to sickness, "Go away. I will rise up by the resurrection life of the Lord." This word is not spoken to God but directly to the mountain. "Be taken up and cast into the sea." This is a prayer with authority.

How can the church have such a prayer with authority? It is by the church having full faith, being without doubt and being clear that what we do is fully according to God's will. Whenever we are not clear about God's will, we do not have faith. Therefore, before we do anything, we have to be clear whether what we are about to do is according to God's will. If it is not God's will, we cannot have faith toward it. If we are not sure that something is God's will, we will not be sure that it can be accomplished. In order to not have any doubt about its accomplishment, we must first have no doubt concerning it being God's will. When we speak carelessly to the mountain, there are no results, because we do not know God's will. But if we have no doubts and are clear about God's will, we can speak boldly to the mountain, "Be taken up and cast into the sea," and the thing will be done. God has commissioned us to be those who issue the command. We command what God has commanded, and we give orders to what God has given orders to. This is a prayer with authority. A prayer with authority is not asking God directly. Rather, it is dealing with problems by directly applying God's authority. All of us have mountains. Of course, these mountains are not the same in size. Our mountain may be this or it may be that. But whatever is blocking us from going on in the spiritual pathway, we can command to go away. This is to pray with authority.

Prayer with authority has much to do with the overcomers. If a Christian does not know this, he cannot be an overcomer. We have to remember that God and the Lord Jesus are on the throne, while the enemy is under the throne. Only prayer can activate the power of God. Nothing can activate God's power except prayer. This is why prayer is indispensable. If one does not pray, he cannot be an overcomer. Only after one knows to pray with authority will he know what prayer is. The most important work of the overcomers is to bring the authority of the throne to earth. Today there is a throne, the throne of God. This throne is ruling, and it is far above everything. In order to have a share in this authority, one must pray. Hence, prayer is very necessary. Those who can move the throne can move everything. We must see that Christ's ascension has made Him far above all things, and we must see that all things are under His feet. For this reason, we can rule over all things with the authority of the throne. All of us have to learn to pray with authority.

How do we practice praying with authority? Let me mention some small things. Suppose a brother has done something wrong, and you want to exhort him. The problem is that you are afraid he will not listen to you. You feel somewhat unsure because you do not know whether he will listen to you. You are afraid that the matter may not be simple to deal with. However, if you pray with authority, you will know how to rule over the situation. You can pray, "Lord, I cannot go to that brother. Please send him to me." From your position on the throne, you can cause him to move. Soon he will come to you personally and tell you, "Brother, I am not clear about a certain matter. Please tell me what to do." Then it will be easy for you to say something to him. This is to pray with authority. You do not do anything according to your strength; you do it by first going through the throne. To pray with authority is not to ask against God's will. It is to know how a thing ought to be done and inform God of what one knows. When that happens, God accomplishes the work.

A prayer with authority rules not only over man but over the weather as well. Müller once had such an experience. He was on his way to Quebec on a ship, and a thick fog came. He told the captain of the ship, "Captain, Saturday afternoon I have to arrive at Quebec." The captain said, "That is impossible." Müller responded, "If your ship cannot take me there on time, God has other ways to take me there." He knelt down and made a very simple prayer. Then he told the captain, "Captain, open the door and see how the fog has cleared." By the time the captain stood up, the fog was cleared away. He was able to be in Quebec as scheduled. This is to pray with authority.

If God is to have a group of overcomers, there must be warfare in prayer. Not only must we war with Satan when we ourselves encounter problems, but also we must rule through the throne when problems arise in our environment. A man cannot be an overcomer on the one hand and fail to be a warrior in prayer on the other hand. If a man wants to be an overcomer, he has to learn to pray with authority.

The church can rule over Hades when it prays with authority. Since Christ has transcended over everything and He is the Head of the church, the church can rule over the demons and everything that belongs to Satan. If the church did not have the authority to rule over the demons and if the Lord had not given this authority to the church, the church could not even survive on earth. The church is able to survive on earth because it has the authority to rule over every satanic thing. Every spiritual man knows that he can deal with the evil spirits with his prayer. We can cast out demons in the name of the Lord, and we can restrain the secret activities of the evil spirits. Satan is very crafty. Not only will he possess man's body with evil spirits, but he will engage in many secret activities. Sometimes he works in man's mind and injects many undesirable thoughts, such as suspicion, fear, disbelief, discouragement, or unfounded and distorted ideas, into man's mind. Through these he deceives and fools man. Sometimes he steals man's word, turning it into a different kind of thought and injecting it into another person's mind. In this way he achieves his goal of causing misunderstanding and stirring up storms. Hence, we have to subdue all the activities of the evil spirits by means of prayer. In our meeting, prayer, or conversation, we must first pray, "Lord, chase away all the evil spirits and do not allow them to do anything here." It is a fact that all the evil spirits are under the feet of the church. If the church exercises authority to pray, it will indeed see the evil spirits being subjected under its feet. This kind of prayer with authority is unlike ordinary begging; it is a command that is based on authority. A prayer with authority is a commanding prayer. It proclaims, "Lord, I will," "Lord, I will not," "Lord, I want this," "Lord, I do not want this," "Lord, I am determined to have this, and

I will not allow that to happen," or "Lord, I only want Your will to be done. I do not want anything else." When we exercise authority this way, we will feel that our prayer has hit our target. If more people rise up to pray this way, many problems in the church will easily be solved. We should exercise dominion through prayer and manage everything in the church through prayer.

We have to see that Christ has ascended. If Christ had not ascended, there would be no way for us to turn. Christ is the Head over all things, and all things are under Him. Christ is the Head of all things to the church. He is the Head of all things on behalf of the church. Since He is the Head of all things on behalf of the church, all things are necessarily under the church. This is something that we have to pay particular attention to.

A prayer with authority has two aspects. One is to bind, and the other is to loose. What is bound on earth will be bound in heaven, and what is loosed on earth will be loosed in heaven. Matthew 18:18 tells us that whatever the earth does, heaven will also do. In verse 19 there is the matter of prayer. Therefore, binding is done through prayer, and loosing is also done through prayer. Both binding prayer and loosing prayer are prayers of authority. Ordinary prayers are prayers that ask God to bind and loose. Prayers with authority are those in which we bind and loose by exercising authority. God binds because the church has bound, and God looses because the church has loosed. God has given this authority to the church. When the church exercises this authority to speak something, God does it.

First let us consider binding prayer. Many people and many things ought to be bound. One brother is very talkative and needs to be bound. You can go to God and pray, "God, do not allow this brother to speak that much. Bind him, Lord, and do not allow him to act this way." When you bind him this way, God in heaven will bind him and stop his speaking. Sometimes someone may interrupt your prayer or your reading of the Word; it may be your wife, husband, children, or friends who are constantly causing the interruption. You can exercise binding prayer against such people. You can say to God, "God, bind this one and do not allow him to interrupt what I am doing." Some brothers speak inappropriate words, but we also have to bind those who quote inappropriate verses and call inappropriate hymns. Such persons should be bound. You may say, "Lord, so-and-so is always causing trouble. Do not allow him to do the same thing again." When you bind in this way, you will see God binding him also. Sometimes people disrupt the peace of the meeting; they may disrupt it through their speaking, crying, or movement in and out of the meeting. You encounter such things frequently. Moreover, it seems that it is always the same ones who are being disruptive. You have to bind such people and things. You may say, "God, we see that these are the ones who are always disrupting the meetings. Bind them and do not allow them to cause any disturbance." You will find that as soon as two or three bind on earth, God will bind in heaven. Not only do you have to bind many interruptions, but you also have to bind many works of the demons. Every time you preach the gospel or testify to someone, the demons work within man's mind to speak many things to him and give him many opposing thoughts. At such times, the church has to bind the evil spirits, stop their speaking, and forbid their work. You may say, "Lord, bind all the works of the evil spirits." If you bind on earth, the matter will be bound in heaven. Many things need to be bound. Many things in our personal life, in the church, in our daily lives, and in our work need to be bound.

The other kind of prayer is the loosing prayer. What do we loose? Some brothers are withdrawn and are afraid to open their mouths to testify or meet people in the meetings. We have to ask God to loose these brothers so that they can be freed from their bondage. Sometimes we should give them a few words of exhortation. But many times, we do not have to say anything; all we have to do is to go to the throne and let the throne take control of them. Many people ought to give up their jobs to serve the Lord. They are bound by their jobs or by other affairs. Some are bound by their families or by unbelieving wives. Some are bound by outward circumstances. There are all kinds of bondage. We can pray to the

Lord to loose them so that they can be released to testify for the Lord. Brothers and sisters, do you see the need for prayers with authority? Do you realize how much prayers with authority should be offered up? Sometimes we have to loose money through our prayer. Satan can easily bind a man's wallet tightly. At times we have to ask God to release the money so that God's work will not suffer through the lack of money. We have to ask God to release us in many things. Furthermore, the truth also needs to be released. We have to tell the Lord all the time, "Lord, release Your truth." Many truths are bound and cannot be released. Many truths have never been heard, and even when they are heard, they are not understood. Hence, we have to ask God to release His truth, so that His truth can run and His children can receive it. In many places the truth cannot break through, and in many places it is impossible for men to receive the truth. We have to ask God to release His truth and set free many churches that are in bondage so that many places which could not receive the truth will be able to receive it. In many places there is no way to pass on the truth. But the Lord has the way. When we pray with authority, the Lord will send the truth there. We have to remember that many things need to be released with prayers of authority.

We have to pay special attention to the binding prayer and loosing prayer. We have to bind many things, and we have to loose many things. We are not begging but binding and loosing with authority. May God be gracious to us so that all of us can learn to pray with authority. Not only do we have to learn to pray, we also have to learn to know the victory of Christ. We have to loose with the victory of Christ, and we have to bind with the victory of Christ. We have to bind all the things that are contrary to God's will. To pray with authority is for heaven to rule on the earth; it is for the earth to exercise the heavenly authority. Every one of us is a man of heaven. As such, we have the authority of heaven. We are merely sojourning on earth today. Everyone who is called by the name of the Lord is His representative on earth. We are God's messengers. We have His life, and we have been transferred from the kingdom of darkness to the kingdom of the Son of His love. This is why we have the heavenly authority. Everywhere we go, we can exercise our heavenly authority. We can rule over the earth through heaven. May God be gracious to us. I hope that we can all be prayer warriors for the Lord and that we will all be overcomers through the authority of Christ so that Christ's victory can be manifested.

Finally, there is a sober warning: we must submit ourselves to God's authority. If we do not submit to God's authority, we cannot pray with authority. Not only must we submit to God's authority with respect to His position, but we also must submit to His authority in our daily living and in all practical matters. Unless we do this, we cannot pray with authority. There was a young brother who was once casting out a demon from a young girl. The demon told the girl to undress herself. The brother commanded the demon with authority, saying, "I command you in the name of Jesus not to undress yourself." The demon immediately said, "All right. If you do not allow me to undress, I will not do it." If the young brother was not victorious in his living, he would have been defeated before the demon. In that case, not only would the demon have ignored his command, but it would have exposed his sins. Brothers and sisters, we know that the whole creation was originally under man's dominion. But the creation is disobedient to man today because man will not obey God's word. The lion slew the man of God because he did not obey God's word (1 Kings 13:20-25). Daniel was not hurt by the lions when he was thrown into the lions' den, because he was innocent before God and he had done no harm before the king. This is why God sent His angel and shut the lions' mouth (Dan. 6:22). A poisonous snake could not hurt the hand of God's faithful servant Paul (Acts 28:3-6), yet worms could kill the proud Herod (12:23). Brothers and sisters, if we submit to God's authority, the demons will be afraid of us and submit to our authority.

The Bible shows us the relationship between prayer, fasting, and authority. Prayer indicates that we seek after God, while fasting indicates that we deny our self. The first right God gave to man was the right to eat. The first thing

God gave to Adam was food. To fast is to renounce one's lawful right. Many Christians only fast but do not deny themselves. In such a case, their fasting cannot be considered fasting. The Pharisees fasted on the one hand and extorted on the other hand (Matt. 23:25). If they were really fasting, they should have returned what they had extorted from others. Prayer is to seek for God, while fasting is to deny the self. We have to seek God and deny the self at the same time. When our pursuit of God and our denial of self is joined and mingled together, immediately there is faith. When we have faith, we have the authority to command the demons to go away. Brothers and sisters, if we seek after God but do not deny our self, we do not have faith, and we do not have authority. But if we seek after God and deny our self, immediately we will have faith and authority and be able to utter prayers of faith and authority. Brothers and sisters, the most important prayers and the most spiritual prayers are prayers of authority.

CHAPTER FIVE

WATCH AND PRAY

"By means of all prayer and petition, praying at every time in spirit and watching unto this in all perseverance and petition concerning all the saints" (Eph. 6:18). We should pay particular attention to the phrase "watching unto this" in this verse. What does "this" refer to? By reading the context we know that it refers to prayer and petition. The apostle said that it is not enough to pray at every time by means of all prayer and petition; we also must be watchful in the matter of prayer and petition. On the one hand we have to pray, and on the other hand, we have to be watchful. What does it mean to be watchful? Being watchful is to be awake and to survey and keep surveillance by keeping one's eyes open. Being watchful is to be on the alert for any danger or emergency. Being watchful in prayer and petition is to have the spiritual insight to discern the stratagems of Satan and to expose his aim and the method of his work. We will mention specifically a few things that we should be watchful in with respect to prayer and petition.

Prayer is a kind of service and should be given the utmost priority. But Satan's strategy is to put everything related to the Lord before prayer and make prayer the least important matter. In spite of the fact that we have been reminded of the importance of the matter over and over again, not many people pay much attention to prayer. Many people are enthusiastic about attending preaching meetings, Bible study meetings, and other meetings of the church. They are interested in these meetings and make the time for these meetings. But whenever there is a prayer meeting, the number is amazingly low. Despite many sermons that remind us that our chief service is prayer and that if we fail in our prayer life, everything else will fail, we still neglect prayer and consider it to be something quite dispensable. Despite the facts that problems are piling up and that we acknowledge with our mouth that prayer is the only way to solve them, we talk more than we pray, and we worry and resort to methods more than we pray. In brief, everything comes before prayer; everything is important. Prayer is always placed last and considered least important. One brother who had a deep knowledge of the Lord once said, "We have all committed the sin of negligence to prayer. We must all say to ourselves: 'You are that man!'" Indeed all of us have to say to ourselves that we are that man! We cannot blame this one and that one for not praying. We ourselves have to repent. We need the Lord to open our eyes to see afresh the importance and value of prayer. At the same time, we have to realize that if we had not been so deceived by Satan, we would not have been so negligent concerning prayer. Therefore, we must be watchful, discover Satan's stratagems, and detect his wiles. We must not allow him to cause us to be relaxed or blind.

After we understand the importance of prayer and have consecrated ourselves to serve and work in prayer, Satan's attacks will come upon us, one after another. We will feel that we cannot find time to pray. While we are intending to pray, someone will knock at our front door or will come to our back door; either the grown-ups will be arguing, or the children will be causing trouble. Either someone will be sick, or someone will encounter some accident. Before we intend to pray, everything is peaceful. When we want to have a specific time of prayer, many matters will immediately come to us, one after another. Many unexpected and unforeseeable things will encroach upon us like an army waiting in ambush. Countless problems will come and stop us from praying. Many things will come our way to try to push away the time for prayer. Do all these things happen accidentally? No, they do not happen accidentally. This is a planned and prearranged strategy of Satan to stop us from praying. He can encourage us to do many things, but he will try to eliminate our time of prayer. He knows that unless spiritual work is built on a foundation of prayer it will not have much value and its eventual result will be failure. Therefore, his strategy is to cause us to become busy in other things and neglect prayer. We are busy in work, visitation, providing hospitality, and preparing sermons. We are busy in the morning and busy in the evening to the extent that prayer is pushed into a corner, and we do not have much time to pray.

Let me quote again the words of the brother who knew the Lord in a deep way.

When the children of Israel planned to leave Egypt, Pharaoh's reaction was to add more burden to their labor. Pharaoh's goal was to make them pay more attention, even all their attention, to their work so that they would not have time to think about leaving Egypt. After you have decided or made plans to have a richer prayer life, Satan will begin a new strategy; he will make you more busy and will pile up work and need upon you so that you will have no time or opportunity to pray. Dear brothers, we must deal with this problem in a definite way. Of course, in fighting for a time of prayer, there may be some dispute concerning our responsibility, duty, and obligations. Some may think that by devoting ourselves to prayer we may neglect our obligations, give up our duty, and damage or hurt our responsibility. However, when we are faced with such situations, we should bring all these problems, that is, our obligations, duty, and responsibility, to the Lord and pray. (However, it is not easy to apply this kind of prayer to every believer. Moreover, this kind of word can often cause misunderstanding because some people are very happy to relinquish their responsibility; they will not seriously take care of their own responsibilities. They will most gladly and easily shuffle their family responsibilities to others in order to have time to pray themselves. May the Lord protect our words so that they will not cause such misunderstanding.) We have to understand that the enemy is trying to use responsibility, obligations, and other matters that touch the conscience, to create the best reason to stop us from praying. If we find that our prayer life has been completely annulled or has fallen into such a confined place that we become completely helpless in living a spiritual and transcendent, overcoming life, under these circumstances, we should pray to the Lord, "Lord, while I pray, I will commit my responsibilities to You. Do not allow anything to frustrate me or damage my time of prayer. Please guard this hour of prayer for me because it is during such time that Your glory is my considera-tion, and do not allow Satan to intrude into this hour." We can also apply the principle of tithing to the matter of prayer. After we have offered to God the portion and position that He deserves and have tithed to God, we will discover that we can more effectively use the other nine-tenths of our time, more so than when we were trying to use all our time for ourselves before tithing it to the Lord. The principle of tithing is very effective. However, we should be aware of the warfare in prayer. We have to stand strongly, powerfully, and firmly upon our position in Christ and should pray according to the victory of the cross. We have to fight for prayer by applying the complete victory the Lord has gained on the cross, and we have to drive out any ground the enemy may have in prayer so that we can garrison our position in prayer. This is like Shammah, one of the mighty men of David, who stood in the midst of the ground full of lentils, defended it, and slew the Philis-tines, and the Lord wrought a great victory (2 Sam. 23:11-12). This ground of lentils signifies our position in prayer; it must be guarded through the victory of Golgotha against the intrusion of the enemy. The kind of warfare that results in prayer is a warfare for prayer. I am afraid that many times we have accepted the environment and considered it impossible to pray at certain times. Because things are happening and developing in a certain way, we think that we cannot pray at that time. Indeed, if we give ground to the devil, things will always come to restrict us from praying. This is the strategy of the devil. We must remove all the hindrances in the battleground of prayer by the Lord's name and according to the victory of His cross. The cross can effectively gain for us the time to pray just as it is effective in other areas, as long as we know how to apply the power of His victory.

The above words can be a great reminder and warning to us. Brothers and sisters, we must fight for the time to pray, and we must secure a time to pray. If we wait until we have time to pray, we will never have the opportunity to pray. We must set aside a time to pray. Andrew Murray said, "Those who do not have a set time to pray do not pray." Hence, we must be watchful and secure the time to pray. We must also guard this time with prayer so that the devil will not usurp it by his deception.

Not only must we be watchful in guarding the time of prayer, but we also must be watchful while we pray, in order that we may pray and have things to pray about. Satan will harass us not only through all kinds of things and outward circumstances that force us to have no time to pray, but even after we actually kneel down to pray he will also use all kinds of deception to frustrate us from prayer. Our minds may be very clear and our thoughts uncluttered before we pray, but as soon as we kneel down to pray, our thoughts become confused. We begin to remember things that we do not need to remember, and we begin to think of things that we do not need to think about ahead of time. Many unnecessary thoughts suddenly come dashing in. Before we pray, none of these things come to us. But as soon as we pray, they come to distract us. Outwardly everything seems peaceful, and there does not seem to be anything to alarm us, but as soon as we kneel down to pray we begin to hear voices in our ear. Actually such strange sounds do not come from outside. These many sounds come in a strange and inexplicable way to disrupt our prayer. We may feel very strong before we pray, but as soon as we kneel down to pray we feel tired and unable to sustain ourselves even though there is no lack of sleep. The tiredness does not come when we do not pray, but as soon as we pray we feel tired and want to sleep. Sometimes even symptoms of a sickness which we did not have before may suddenly come upon us. We may want to discharge a burden through prayer, but when we kneel down to pray we cannot offer a single word. It seems as if we are choked and short of prayer. It is obvious that there are many things we should pray about, but as soon as we start praying, we become numb and cold and do not feel we have anything to pray about. Even when we pray, it is like speaking to the air, and we run out of things to say in two or three sentences. None of the above conditions were with us before we began to pray. Only after we kneel down to pray do they suddenly come upon us. If we do not realize that this is Satan's deception to destroy our prayer, we will want to stop praying and stand up soon after we kneel down. Therefore, in order to pray, to pray thoroughly and release our burden through prayer, we have to be watchful in our prayer. We have to be watchful to withstand the situations that would stop us from praying. This requires us to fight the battle. Before we pray, we must pray that God will enable us to pray. While we pray, we have to ask God to keep us undistracted in prayer and deliver us from all the deception of the enemy that stops us from praying. We have to speak to all the distracting thoughts and voices as well as all the weakness and sickness and declare that all these inexplicable happenings are lies and deceptions of Satan and that we oppose them. We have to open our mouth and chase them away. We should not give them any ground; we should be watchful to withstand the wiles of Satan through prayer. Then not only will we be able to pray, we will be able to pray thoroughly.

In order to pray thoroughly and powerfully we cannot just hope vainly. We cannot glide comfortably into this prayer life, and we cannot follow our imagination to drift into this prayer life. We must learn, we must be broken, and we must fight before we can secure this kind of prayer.

During our prayer, we must also guard against the prayers that are not prayers. Satan will not only take away our time of prayer, but also strip us of the strength to pray. He will come in even while we pray to make us speak many unrelated, confused, unimportant, and vain words. He will cause us to ask in vain and to waste our time of prayer. He will try to occupy our time of prayer so that the effect of our prayer will amount to nothing. Many fleshly, old, long, mundane, heartless, and aimless prayers are time-consuming and wasteful prayers. It may seem that we are praying out of habit, but actually within these prayers there are suggestions, instigations, and deceptions of Satan. If we are not watchful, our prayer will become meaningless and fruitless. One brother mentioned a story he read in the biography of Evan Roberts. Once a few people were in his home praying for something. Halfway through one brother's prayer, Mr. Roberts went over and covered that brother's mouth, saying, "Brother, don't go on. You are not praying." The brother reading this story said within himself, "How could Mr. Roberts do this?" But later he realized that Mr. Roberts was right. Many words in our prayers are spoken by the flesh through the instigation of Satan. These prayers may be long, but many of them are impractical and useless. Brothers and sisters, this is a fact. Many times in our prayer, we seem to circle around the whole world. Time is wasted and strength is exhausted, yet nothing that is to the point is prayed about. We cannot expect God to answer this kind of prayer. This kind of prayer does not have any spiritual value. Hence, when we pray, we have to be watchful and not spend too much time or give too many reasons. Rather, we should speak what is in our heart to God in a sincere way. We must never fill up our prayer with many empty words.

We have to be watchful that when we pray we do not speak loosely. A man who was very experienced in prayer once wrote a hymn. In that hymn one line talks about prayer. It says that if one wants to pray to God he should first be well prepared about what he wants from God. Brothers and sisters, when we kneel down to pray, if we do not know what we want, how can we expect God to answer our prayer? If our prayer is aimless and heartless, it is not a prayer. Satan will utilize this and make us think we have prayed. Actually we have not prayed at all. We must be watchful and on guard. Every time that we come to pray before God, we must know what we want in our heart. If we do not have any desire, we do not have prayer. All prayers are governed by our desire. Our Lord pays attention to this. The blind man Bartimaeus beseeched the Lord, saying, "Jesus, Son of David, have mercy on me!" The Lord asked him, "What do you want Me to do for you?" (Mark 10:47, 51). The Lord is asking today: "What do you want Me to do for you?" Can you answer this question? Some brothers and sisters pray for ten or twenty minutes. Afterward, when you call them and ask, "What were you asking God for?", they may not be able to tell you anything. Although they may have said much in their prayer, they do not even know what they were asking. This is a prayer without a desire. It is an aimless prayer and one that is not counted in God's sight. We have to be watchful to guard against this kind of prayer.

When we pray, there must be not only the desire but also the word to express the desire. Sometimes in our desire we have something we want, but the more we speak the further away we seem to be from our desire. We must also be watchful to guard against this. Satan's strategy is either to hold us back so that we do not pray or push us forward while we pray so that the more we pray the more we are lost. Therefore, when we pray we have to guard ourselves so that our words will not deviate from the center. Once we discover that our words have deviated, we should come back. We must be watchful to aim in the right direction and persist to keep out unnecessary words. We have to guard ourselves from praying the prayers that are not prayers at all.

We must be watchful in prayer and not allow Satan to disrupt our prayer with his deception. Satan will often accuse us after we fail a little and cause us to analyze ourselves while we pray so that we cannot open our mouth to God. When God's answer seems to be far away, Satan will cause us to become disappointed and discouraged, and he will take away our strength to wait on God. Brothers and sisters, if our prayer is to be according to God's will, we have to persist in our prayer until the end. Even when we fail, we can come before God through the blood of the Lamb; there is no need for Satan to interfere with us. We have to be like the widow who prayed until the judge had to avenge her (Luke 18:7). We have to be like the Shunammite who would not leave Elisha until he went with her (2 Kings 4:30). We believe that a delay in answers to prayer can help us know something we did not know before, and it can help us learn lessons we were ignorant of. We must never allow Satan to cut off our prayer or damage it.

Here we can sing more hymns concerning spiritual warfare, such as hymns #880, 775, 876, and 893.

When a few of us pray together, Satan will not let us go easily. He will be active in many ways and devise many plans to stop such prayers. There may be unfounded rumors, untrue reports, jealousies without reasons, complicated misunderstandings, inexplicable fear, and waves of threats that seem to come from nowhere. All these are under the secret direction of Satan for the purpose of creating some kind of division to shake the gathering of prayer and destroy this prayer in oneness. Therefore, brothers and sisters, we must "prove all things" (1 Thes. 5:21). We must not believe in anything lightly, be shaken lightly, nor pass on words lightly. If we are watchful, we will find that many unnecessary, inaccurate words and things are deceptions from the enemy. His goal is to make God's people fearful, weak, and even dispersed. Therefore, on the one hand, we must pray, and on the other hand, we must be on guard. We must follow the example of Nehemiah, who set a watch day and night (Neh. 4:9). Our answer to Satan's threat is: "There are no such things done as thou sayest, but thou feignest them out of thine own heart....Should such a man as I flee? and who is there, that, being as I am, would go into the temple to save his life? I will not go in" (Neh. 6:8, 11). We will not fear, and we will not stop praying. One brother said, "How much we need a watchman to guard against the deception of the devil, for the ways he uses to destroy the corporate life of God's people are far beyond our ability to count and enumerate." For this reason, we must be watchful to examine and oversee these things so that Satan will not have the opportunity to divide us, destroy our oneness in prayer, or cut off our prayers.

We must also be watchful in our prayer so that we do not fall under Satan's deception of not making our prayer specific. There are often many things that need to be decided, many people that need to be prayed for, many central messages that need to be released, and many problems that need to be solved. However, when we pray, we seem to be short of something to pray for. There are not even words for our prayer, and we barely manage to finish two or three sentences. We have to know that Satan's attack is present. It is true that through our laziness, fear of entanglement, lack of love, or unwillingness to advance and be thorough our prayers sometimes become routine. But many times when we gather together we truly want to pray. Yet very few prayers are offered. This proves that something menacing is present. This something is Satan's design to stop us from praying. If we are watchful, we will find that many cases of forgetfulness, oversight, procrastination, and carelessness did not happen intentionally. Rather, Satan is dragging us down, deceiving us, stealing from us, and robbing us. Therefore, we have to oppose his strategies. We have to pray thoroughly for people, for things, for the truth, and for our problems. Brothers and sisters, we have to realize that a hasty, "economical" prayer is often a careless prayer that will give ground to Satan. We must not let go, and we must ask the Lord to remind us of all the burdens in our prayer and give us the utterance to pray them. At the same time, we have to deal with our own slothfulness and procrastination. Our Lord rose "very early in the morning...and...prayed." When Simon and those with him hunted for Him and told Him, "All are seeking You," His answer was, "Let us go elsewhere...that I may preach there also, because for this purpose I came out" (Mark 1:35-38). How specific and thorough is our Lord. He "went out to the mountain to pray, and He spent the whole night in prayer to God. And when it became day, He called His disciples to Him, and He chose from them twelve, whom He also named apostles" (Luke 6:12-13). How specific and thorough this is. When the apostle Paul reminded the Ephesian saints to be watchful in prayer and petition, he mentioned "petition concerning all the saints, and for me, that utterance may be given to me in the opening of my mouth, to make known in boldness the mystery of the gospel...that in it I would speak boldly, as I ought to speak" (Eph. 6:18-20). This is also very specific and clear; it is something that requires much petitioning. If we have a Body consciousness and if we are concerned for the sinners' souls, for the saints' affairs, and for the service of the Lord's servants, there will be countless things and people that we have to make petition for. There must also be numerous prayers for every truth to be released. In writing to the Ephesian saints, the apostle Paul said, "For this cause I bow my knees unto the Father…that He would grant you, according to…" (3:14-16). Here we see that Paul's revelation of glorious truth came from prayer and that the revelation itself is prayer. From this we see that the true worth of the light of the truth comes by prayer. We should pray the truth into our lives and then pray it out. We should pray over all the truths that we have heard and spoken, so that these truths do not remain merely in our mind or in our notebooks, but are manifested in our lives. How many definite and thorough prayers are needed for this!

The devil's attachment and manipulation are behind many problems. If we are not watchful, we will think that there are only problems with people, things, and events. But if we have spiritual insight, we will see that the work of the devil is present, and we will cast out all the demons behind these things. Sometimes, as the Lord said, a demon "does not go out except by prayer and fasting" (Matt. 17:21). This requires us to be watchful on the one hand and persist in prayer on the other hand. Otherwise, the difficulty will be like a mountain; either we have to command it to move to the sea, or we have to walk around it. Brothers and sisters, let us wake up. We have to pray in a thorough way. We must expose the deception of Satan and destroy all that he attaches himself to and manipulates. We must cast out the demons behind all the problems.

Not only do we have to be watchful before we pray and while we pray, we also have to be watchful after we pray. We must be watchful to examine all the changes that happen after we pray. We must realize that all serious prayers and prayers with burden are made not only "by means of all prayer" but also "at every time." It is not once but many times. And it is not once by means of all prayer but at every time by means of all prayer. Therefore, we have to take note of any new development, changes, or movement after every prayer. For example, when Elijah prayed on Mount Carmel, he knelt down and put his face between his knees. He also asked his servant to look at the sea seven times until the servant reported that he saw a little cloud arising out of the sea like a man's hand. Then he asked his servant to tell Ahab to prepare his chariot and go down so that the rain would not stop him (1 Kings 18:42-44). This can also be seen from Elisha praying for the Shunammite woman's child. He stretched himself upon the child until the flesh of the child became warm. Then he returned and walked in the house to and fro, went up, and stretched himself upon the child until the child sneezed seven times and opened his eyes. Then he delivered the child to the mother (2 Kings 4:33-37). Whether Elijah or Elisha, they did not just kneel down to pray without asking for anything. While they were praying they were observing the effect of prayer and the changes in the environment. For example, you may be praying for someone who opposes the Lord. You pray that God will make him believe. You may pray for him by means of all prayer, and you may have God's promise for this. But the outward circumstance may appear to be worse; he may become stronger in his opposition. If you ignore this and continue to pray the same prayer, it is not enough. You must detect this and tell it to the Lord. If you are watchful, you will receive light from Him. You may realize that your prayer has affected him, and you can begin praising God. Or you may change your prayer and cast another net. Perhaps, after some time, he will soften, and you can then change to another kind of prayer to cast another net. We have to adjust our prayer according to the situation. To do this we need to be watchful.

Ephesians 6 is a chapter on spiritual warfare. The most important thing in this chapter is the prayer mentioned at the end. Among God's children, prayer is the one thing that is most easily attacked. This is why we must be watchful to fight for a time to pray, to guard prayer, to stop prayers that are not prayer, and to be on guard against Satan's strategy to cut off our prayer. We must remember that prayer is a service, an excellent service. We have to watch and pray, and we must practice conscientiously, so that Satan will not have the opportunity to destroy our prayer.